A Co   , on
ROMANS

UNLOCKING THE NEW TESTAMENT

A Commentary on
ROMANS

David Pawson

Anchor Recordings

First published under this title in Great Britain in 2013
This revised and updated edition published in 2015 by
Anchor Recordings Ltd
72 The Street, Kennington, Ashford TN24 9HS

For more of David Pawson's teaching, including DVDs and CDs, go to www.davidpawson.com

FOR FREE DOWNLOADS: www.davidpawson.org

For further information,
email info@davidpawsonministry.com

ISBN 978-1-909886-78-0

Contents

This book is based on a series of talks. Originating as it does from the spoken word, its style will be found by many readers to be somewhat different from my usual written style. It is hoped that this will not detract from the substance of the biblical teaching found here.

As always, I ask the reader to compare everything I say or write with what is written in the Bible and, if at any point a conflict is found, always to rely upon the clear teaching of scripture.

David Pawson

OUTLINE OF
THE LETTER TO THE ROMANS

RIGHT(EOUS) RELATIONSHIPS

A. VERTICAL: WITH GOD (1-8) Salvation worked in
    1. SIN AND WRATH (1-3a)
        a. Gentile – 'they' (1)
        b. Jewish – 'you' (2)
        c. Gentile and Jew – 'we' (3a)

    2. JUSTIFICATION (3b-5)
        a. Faith of Jew and Gentile – Jesus (3b)
        b. Father of Jew and Gentile – Abraham (4)
        c. Fall of Jew and Gentile – Adam (5)

    3. SANCTIFICATION (6-8)
        a. Licence – Gentile (6)
        b. Legalism – Jew (7)
        c. Liberty – Spirit (8)

B. HORIZONTAL: WITH PEOPLE (9-16) Salvation worked out
    1. ISRAEL AND CHURCH (9-11)
        a. Selected in past (9)
        b. Stumbling in present (10)
        c. Saved in future (11)

    2. CHURCH AND STATE (12-13)
        a. Church (12)
            i. Internal harmony
            ii. External hostility
        b. State (13)
            i. Political duty accepted
            ii. Moral depravity rejected

    3. JEW AND GENTILE (14-16)
        a. Jewish scruples and Gentiles (14-15a)
        b. Jewish apostles and Gentiles (15b)
        c. Jewish believers and Gentiles (16)

In the summer of 386 AD, a North African who was now a professor of rhetoric in Milan sat weeping in the garden of his friend. While he was brilliant intellectually, he was living an immoral life. His friend had just pleaded with him to give it all up and turn over a new leaf. While he sat there, weeping because he felt too weak to break his habits, he heard a child in a neighbour's garden singing, "Take up and read, take up and read."

Lying by his side was a scroll his friend had been reading. He picked it up and read. It happened to be Paul's letter to the Romans, and this is what he read from that letter: "Let us conduct ourselves becomingly as in the day. Not in revelry and drunkenness, not in debauchery and licentiousness, not in quarrelling and jealousy, but put on the Lord Jesus Christ and make no provision for the flesh, to gratify its desires" (Romans 13:13–14). He wrote, "No further would I read, nor had I any need. Instantly, at the end of this sentence a clear light flooded my heart and all the darkness of doubt vanished away." His name was Augustine, and he was one of the greatest Christians there has ever been. His experience of reading Romans led to his becoming a bishop of Hippo (in North Africa). He became known to most people as the great *Saint* Augustine.

Then there was Martin Luther, an Augustinian monk and professor in Wittenberg, Germany, who gave lectures on Romans. That was a crucial part of his conversion and the beginning of the Protestant Reformation.

One of the great New Testament commentators was a man called Bengel, and he called Romans his "holiday book" because whenever he went on a holiday he took it with him. John Wesley was converted through someone reading aloud Luther's preface to Romans. William Tyndale, who gave us the first English Bible, on which the King James Version was based, said this is the most excellent part of the New Testament. I could go on quoting person after person in church history who owed so much to this very long letter. It is not only the longest letter Paul wrote, it is the longest one in the New Testament and the longest letter we have discovered from the ancient world. That is why it takes quite a time to read it and, above all, to teach it.

The Letter to the Romans has had more effect on the church over the centuries than any other part of the New Testament. Chrysostom, one of the Church Fathers, who lived in Bethlehem, used to say that this book ought to be read to you aloud twice a week and it will then make you a good Christian.

We begin with some basic questions: who, where and why? Paul the missionary, formerly Saul of Tarsus, wrote the letter. But actually he did not write it, he dictated it, as he did most of his letters, to a secretary or "amanuensis" as they called them. In this case that was Tertius, whom Paul mentions at the end of the letter. A lady brought this letter to Rome. Her name was Phoebe, and she is especially mentioned first in the last chapter of greetings. The church in Rome was told to welcome her. Little did she know what she was carrying in her hand all the way from Corinth to Rome! Where was it sent to? The church in Rome. Where was it sent from? A place called Cenchreae, which was the worst part of Corinth, the red-light district there. That is where Phoebe came from. I don't know what she was in her previous life, but she was now a deaconess.

The next question, and the most important, is this: why was it written? This is the key question for every book in the Bible. Don't try to understand any biblical book until you are able to answer this question. That will be the key that unlocks it for you. I have written a book entitled *Unlocking the Bible*, in which I write about every book in the Bible and tell you why it was written. With Romans we have a problem. The letter does not include the reason why it was written, and we have to read between the lines and guess. That is why the commentators all seem to have a different explanation as to why Paul wrote such a long letter. I believe the reasons they offer are wrong, but let us think about one or two of them. Many say it was because he needed room. Some said he was planning to go west to the other half of the Mediterranean after having evangelised the eastern half, and that he needed a new base. Antioch could be too far away. Others have said that Rome would make a good base for the west, so he is writing to encourage the believers in Rome to be his new base. Others say he had always had an ambition to preach his gospel in the metropolis, the very centre of the Roman Empire. Not being able to do that since he was on his way to Jerusalem, he sent a letter containing his gospel for their encouragement and even approval. I don't think that is why he wrote this letter. The real reason is that Rome needed Paul. You did not write letters lightly in the ancient world because there was no easy postal service. You had to have a very good reason for writing, and I think you find that reason in Rome itself.

I will give you my own explanation of why it was written and let you judge for yourself. A devastating situation had arisen in the Roman church, which had gone through four different phases. It began as a Jewish church. No apostle went to Rome to found it. There were people from Rome on the day of Pentecost, Jews having come for the great Feast in Jerusalem. They went back to Rome, and I believe this church was the result of their having been present at Pentecost. It began as a totally Jewish church. But Rome was the capital of a conglomerate empire of many ethnic groups and, after a while, Gentiles began to be interested, so it became, secondly, a church which was a mixture of Jewish and Gentile members.

Then came the emperor Claudius. During his reign in Rome he had to deal with a lot of civic unrest, which seems to have happened among the Jews in Rome, of whom there were forty thousand in those days. The historical records tell us that the unrest arose over someone called "Chrestos", which is probably the Roman name for Christ, and that therefore the Jews in Rome were being stirred up as they had been all around the empire. Wherever Paul went, he upset as many Jews as he got converted. Here we have the same thing happening again. Claudius, quite an immature emperor, said, "All Jews must leave Rome," and he banished them. You read about that in Acts 18. When Claudius said that every Jew had to leave Rome, that included the believing Jews. Those who believed in *Yeshua HaMashiach* were kicked out along with all the other Jews. Then, of course, the Roman church became a totally Gentile church.

So there had been: stage one, a totally Jewish church; stage two, a mixed church of Jews and Gentiles; stage three, a totally Gentile church. Stage four came when the next emperor, Nero, invited the Jews back to Rome for economic reasons. They had been running businesses in Rome which had now collapsed. Nero in his early years was quite a good emperor. Just as Hitler in his early years did a lot for Germany and stopped the inflation, got the Volkswagen car built, and built the autobahns. Nero did much the same. But, in the same way, power went to his head and finally there was a great fire in Rome which people blamed Nero for starting. They knew he had ambitions for the heart of Rome, to rebuild it in magnificent style, so they thought, "Who burned down the centre of Rome? Why, Nero did, so that he could rebuild it." Nero looked around for a scapegoat, saw the Christians and blamed them. That is when the first horrible persecution broke out for Christians. Here are just two of the things he did: he would get wild animals, kill them, skin them, and then tie the skins around Christians and set other wild animals on them and enjoy the fun. I have stood in the back garden of his palace and remembered that Christians were covered in pitch and set alight and tied to posts in his garden to light his garden parties. This was the hated Nero.

The letter to the Romans was written before Nero did all that, before that persecution broke out. So what went wrong? For me, this explains the whole letter. When the Jewish believers came back to the Roman church by permission of Nero, the Gentile church would not receive them. They were not welcomed back because a belief had arisen which we now call "replacement theology". It is everywhere in the churches in my country. It was the belief that when the Jews were banished under Claudius, the hand of God was in that. He was punishing them for their rejection of Jesus. The Jews were no longer his chosen people and had been replaced by the church. That idea had got a deep hold in the church of Rome. Now many of the Jewish believers who came back under Nero were friends and even relatives of Paul, among them two tent makers with whom he had worked in Corinth. Aquila and Priscilla came back to Rome and then immediately realised that Jews were not welcomed in the church that had originally been a Jewish church. The teaching was that God himself had now rejected the Jews and replaced them with the Gentile church.

That is why, in the middle of the letter, Paul reaches the climax and the point of the whole letter in chapter 11. He gradually builds up to that, as we shall see. Chapter 11 begins with the question "Has God rejected the Jews?" Our polite English versions say something like, "on no account", or words to that effect. Actually, it is a very strong negative statement, the strongest negative in the Greek language, and it should be translated "Never!" Had the Jews fallen so far that they cannot recover? Never! That is a favourite expression of Paul's and it appears more than in just those two instances in the letter, but that is the heart of it.

What he is fighting for is a church at the heart of the empire that includes Jew and Gentile; one new man in Christ Jesus. That is Paul's heart. Not only did all roads lead to Rome, all roads went out from Rome. News went out along those roads, and if he could not get the Jew and Gentile together in one fellowship under one Saviour and one Lord, that was going to spread a gigantic split in the early Christian church right through the Roman Empire.

Paul was in a dilemma. He was on his way to Jerusalem to take some money from Gentile converts to the Jews of Jerusalem. He could not go to Rome, and he was so frustrated. What could he do? He could write to them. That was the best thing he could do. That explains this very long letter because it was a church he had not founded and had never been to – a church that would not recognise him. They would have heard about him and the troubles he got into wherever he went, so he was faced with a difficult task. Somehow he must tackle this basic problem, but he could not go headlong into it as he did in Galatians, where within a few verses of the opening remarks he was blazing with fury about what was happening in Galatia. But Galatia was one of his babies. It was a church he had founded. Rome was not, so he had to pause and consider: how can I approach this basic problem without upsetting them straightaway, without saying the wrong thing too early? So he spends at least ten chapters leading up to what he wants to say.

The reason why most commentators have missed this reason for the writing of the letter is quite simple. They have concentrated on chapters 1–8 and 12–16. Most preachers preach from those, the beginning and the end of the letter, and somehow have dismissed chapters 9–11 as a kind of intrusion, a "bee in the bonnet" belonging to Paul that he just wanted to get off his chest about Israel. Therefore the chapters in the heart of the letter, which are its climax of the letter and reason, have been quietly put aside.

Most have concentrated on chapters 1–8. When I was studying theology at Cambridge, two of my tutors were C.H. Dodd and the Bishop of Woolwich, John A. T. Robinson, an infamous bishop who wrote "Honest to God". John Robinson, was my tutor for Romans. He carefully took us through 1–8 and then stopped. The rest of the Epistle was not part of the syllabus for a degree and so he concentrated on the first eight chapters, which people have done since the Reformation. Luther concentrated on 1–8 and therefore never really understood the reason why the whole letter was written. Without chapters 9–11 (particularly 11), the book does not make any sense.

This letter is not Paul's gospel. If you take your gospel from Romans then you will miss out on some vital truths that Paul always included when he preached. Take one example—repentance. There is nothing about repentance in the whole letter to the Romans, and if you base your gospel on Romans you will not preach repentance. There is nothing in Romans about the future, about the second coming of Christ, which was always part of Paul's gospel. Romans is only about those bits of the gospel that are relevant to the Jewish-Gentile relationship. That is one of the most important things to underline. Paul does pick out certain truths of the gospel very strongly, like justification by faith, but only because that is going to build the relationship between Jew and Gentile. These words – Jew and Gentile –run all the way through the whole book.

By the way, I'm sure you know that God never intended his written word to be divided into chapters and verses.

The chapters were the idea of an English Archbishop of Canterbury, who in the thirteenth century decided to divide God's word up into chapters and number them. A French printer, who was riding in a carriage from Paris to Lyon and was a bit bored, took his Bible and divided the chapters into verses, giving them numbers. We are so used to quoting chapter and verse numbers that we have changed the word "text" which originally in English meant the content of a whole book. The text of the book was everything in it. Now the word "text" means one sentence in a book, and we have become text-quoting people. Nearly always we quote texts out of context. Many Christians can quote John 3:16, but far fewer know 3:17. I wonder whether many know the meaning of one word in John 3:16, the word "so". What do you think that means? It does not mean God sooo loved the world, or so much, so deeply. It doesn't mean that at all. It means thus; it means in the same way; even so. That's what it really means, and when you check up in 3:14–15, the same word is used. "As Moses lifted up the serpent in the wilderness, even so must the Son of Man be lifted up." That is what it means – in the same way. You only get that meaning from verses 14–15. John 3:16 is telling you: "In the same way, God loved the world when he gave his only begotten Son." In the same way as what? Well, verses 14–15 tell you. It was when God killed hundreds of Hebrew people, his own people, because they grumbled about the food he gave them. He sent a plague of poisonous snakes. Hundreds died, and they realised that it was God sending the snakes. They said: Moses, go and tell God we're sorry that we grumbled about the food. Moses said: Please God, take the snakes away. They're sorry they grumbled about the manna. God's answer was: No, I'm not going to take the snakes away, but I'll give you a cure for snakebite. Make a metal snake, put it up on the pole, and anybody who is bitten by a poisonous snake, if they go to the hill outside the camp and look at that pole and the metal snake on it then the poison will leave their system. In other words, there will still be death from the snakes unless they go and look at the bronze snake on the pole. "Even so," says John, "God loved the world." He doesn't take death away from the world, but he says go and look at the cross; go and look at Jesus lifted up and the poison will leave you, and you will have eternal life. Do you make sense of it now? Do you see what we have missed by taking text out of context?

That is just a little aside, because I am basically a contextual Bible teacher. I don't quote a lot of chapter and verse numbers. I want my hearers and readers to go and search the scriptures not look them up. If you hear a preacher who gives you every text reference he has in his notes, you will maybe go home and look them up by chapter and verse. I would rather tell you to go and search the scripture as the Bereans did and see if what I am telling you is so. Do not believe anything I tell you unless you can find it in your Bible for yourself. I am not infallible. Check me out, especially with Romans.

Here is a brief outline of the whole letter showing you how Jew-Gentile relationships are the key to everything Paul has written in this letter.

If you want a title for Romans I would say Right Relationships, but for "right" in the Bible you usually see the word "righteous". Therefore the whole letter is about righteous relationships between Jew and Gentile. How does he deal with that? Most letters of Paul begin with belief and then in the latter half go on to behaviour – doctrine first, then duty. That is always the right Christian order. Some people try to start by behaving like a Christian without having been converted. They become do-gooders. They are beginning at the wrong end of the whole process. You begin with doctrine. You begin with what you believe, and then you go on to how to behave as a Christian. So in Ephesians, chapters 1–3 is what to believe, and chapters 4–6 how to behave. In the same way, chapters 1–8 of Romans concerns your vertical relationship with God. That must be put right first, and then in the second half he deals with your horizontal relationships with each other. The first part I call Salvation Worked In – that is by God. The second half is Salvation Worked Out. I am basing that on the verse in Philippians that says, "Work out your own salvation, for it is God who's worked in you." God working in you first and you working it out secondly is the order in the Christian life.

Paul talks about the vertical relationship with God under three headings. In chapter 1 to the first part of chapter 3 he talks about the sins of men and the wrath of God which is resting on them. We will look at this in detail below, but he begins with Gentile sin, which is very blatant and open. He tells us how Gentiles sin, but he is very tactful. He doesn't say, "You Gentiles." He understands that they have all left that behind when they became Christians. He talks about "they" and "them" in the third person, referring to the immoral Gentile world. Then in chapter two he changes the pronoun to "you". He is now talking to Jews and their secret sins. Gentiles openly sin; Jews secretly sin. They become, as Jesus called them, "whitewashed tombs." Then he puts them both together and says, "We all of us, Jew and Gentile, we are sinners." So he has convicted Gentiles of sin, then the Jews, and then all together; all have sinned. That makes sense. Gentile and Jew are on an equal basis in sin.

Then he turns to justification in the second half of chapter 3, through to chapter 5. He talks about the faith the Jew and Gentile need in Jesus to be justified. Then in chapter 4 he talks about another man, Abraham, and shows how Abraham is the father of Jew and Gentile, not just the circumcised but the uncircumcised. Then he talks about the fall of Jew and Gentile in Adam. So he is saying that Jew and Gentile are united in Christ, they are united in Abraham, and they are united in Adam. They are together – together in sin; together in justification.

Paul moves on to sanctification in chapters 6–8 and he is telling them now about the danger of backsliding, of failing to reach the goal of sanctification. He is now saying: our backsliding will be different. Gentiles go back into licence (chapter 6); Jews go back into legalism (chapter 7), and they both need the life of liberty in the Spirit. We will look at these matters in more detail. That is an outline of the vertical relationship with God, a righteous God – a right relationship, a righteous relationship.

Then Paul turns to the horizontal – the relationships with each other, working out our salvation. In chapters 9–11 we learn of the relationship between the church and Israel. That is a vital relationship, and we will go through that too in detail because as I have pointed out, many churches and preachers rather leave 9–11 on one side while the Christian Zionists give us an overdose of them. On the whole, Calvinists love chapter 9, Evangelicals love chapter 10 and Zionists love chapter 11. I wish they would get all three chapters into their minds. There is a vital horizontal relationship between Jew and Gentile, between Israel and the church. "Our future is bound up with each other," says Paul. The future of the church is the future of Israel too, and vice versa.

Then Paul writes about the relationships between church and state because he is writing to the church in Rome, which is the headquarters of the empire, the centre of government. So he talks in chapter 12 about the relationships within the church and the relationships with those who persecute the church. You can expect and hope for harmony inside the church, but you can expect hostility outside. He shows you how to deal with both. Chapter 13 is on the Christian relationship to the state. That is a vital insight. Notice that the state in that chapter is not a democracy, yet we are told there to pay our taxes, to pray for the state and so on. Many Christians need to learn particularly the word he gives – respect for the state. If you join in mockery of politicians you are going directly against Paul's letter to the Romans. If you make fun of politicians and pull them down to your level, then that is what you are doing. You are disobeying Romans. As far as the state is concerned we are to accept their political duty but to reject their moral depravity. That is a delicate balance to keep.

Finally, the letter goes on to particular relationships between Jew and Gentile. In chapters 14–15 the teaching about the relationship between strong and weak Christians refers to believing Jews and believing Gentiles and tells you how that relationship should be. Then he moves on to the question of Jewish apostles and their effect on the Gentile world. He cites Jesus as the apostle to Jews, and yet it was for the Gentiles as well; and himself as the Jew of Jews and his burden to all the Gentiles.

Chapter 16 is nothing but greetings, yet at the heart of it, having listed the Jews in Rome, he tells the Gentile believers to kiss them. That is a real shock. Can you imagine telling a whole lot of Gentiles to go and kiss the Jews? Well, that is what he told them! "Greet one another with a holy kiss." Do you know the difference between a holy and an unholy kiss? Two minutes! There are other differences, which we will come to later.

This has been a very simple outline of the whole letter to show you that the Jewish-Gentile tension underlies it. Chapter 11 is the climax of the letter in which Paul rebukes Gentile believers for their arrogance toward his own Jewish people.

1. INTRODUCTION

ROMANS 1:1–17

A. 1-7 PAUL'S MISSION (he, we, you)
  1. 1-4 CALLED BY GOD
    a. 1 APOSTLE – obeyed in faith
    b. 2-4 GOSPEL – promised in scriptures (O.T.)
      i. Son of David – human descendant – incarnation
      ii. Son of God – divine declaration – resurrection
  2. 5-7 CALLED TO GENTILES
    a. ALL GENTILES in world
    b. YOU TOO in Rome
      i. Beloved by God as sons
      ii. Belonging to God as saints

B. 8-17 PAUL'S MOTIVATION ("I" 12x)
  1. 8-10 His INTERCESSION (I remember you)
    a. Thanking: heard - famous faith
    b. Petition: see - for himself
  2. 11-13 His AMBITION (I long to see you)
    a. Believers – impart spiritual gifts. Encouragement
    b. Unbelievers – have a harvest. Evangelism
  3. 14-15 His OBLIGATION (I am bound)
    a. Greeks educated   wise
    b. Non-Greeks uneducated   foolish   Rome both
  4. 16-17 His SATISFACTION (I am not ashamed)
    a. 16 Power of God
      i. Salvation for all believers
      ii. Jew first, then Gentile
    b. 17 Righteousness from God
      i. Faith, first to last
      ii. Scripture (Habakkuk 2:4)

PLEASE READ ROMANS 1:1–17

This is Paul's introduction of himself to the believers in Rome. Since he has never been there, they do not know him directly as an apostle. He has to introduce himself to them, which he does in a very skilful way. How to introduce himself to the unknown believers of Rome? He does this in two major ways. First, he tells them about his mission. Secondly, he invites them into his own heart, his motivation. In my outlines I break up a passage to see which are the main points, which are the sub-points and which are the minor points under each heading, breaking it up so that we can grasp what Paul is saying. A dear old lady came to me once and said, "David, what I like about your preaching is that you break it up small enough for me to digest it." I thanked her for that compliment, but we should all be doing that—breaking it down all the way into little bits, so that we can take a bite at a time and digest the whole thing.

First, Paul's *mission*. He describes himself in most amazing ways. In vv. 1–7 it is all in impersonal, third-person pronouns. He talks about "he", "we" and "you", but does not use the word "I" when talking about his mission. When he gets to his *motivation* the word "I" comes all the way through, so "I" becomes a key word in the second part of this passage, 1–17. Whereas the first part is general and he is almost writing as if he is someone else and describing them objectively, he then comes to very subjective "I" and starts talking about his inner feelings.

The first thing he calls himself is a servant of Christ Jesus only he didn't use the word servant. He used a much stronger word, *doulos*, which means a slave of Christ Jesus.

We are used to living in a world without slavery, but it is still around. When I was a chaplain in the RAF, I found that there are still slaves being sold and bought in the Middle East, but it has been banned from the Western world for a long time now. Slavery is used frequently in this letter as a picture of us. When we get to chapter 6, Paul says there is no such thing as freedom. You are a slave all your life. You are born into slavery—slavery to sin—and the result is death. A Christian is someone who has changed masters and changed one slavery for another. Christians are slaves. It means that you have no time of your own, no money of your own, no possessions of your own. They all belong to your master, and Jesus said whoever sins is a slave of sin. When you are converted you change slavery: from a slavery to sin to a slavery of righteousness; from slavery to the devil to slavery to the Lord; from slavery to death to slavery to life. Which slavery do you want? You can only have one or the other.

Now that is a way of talking which we can hardly use today. It is simply not politically correct to say "I'm a slave", but Paul had no hesitation. He had been bought with a price. The life he now lived he did not live himself—Christ lived in him. His whole life belonged to someone else now, and we need to remember that. Some people think that if they have given a tithe to the church the rest of the money is theirs to do what they like with. Actually the new covenant does not teach tithing, it teaches 100% of your money belongs to the Lord. Everything you have belongs to the Lord now. You do not have any rights of your own now. What a way to talk! How to be a popular preacher – preach Romans 6 on slavery! We will return to that.

Paul says, "I'm a slave of Jesus," not a servant, but we want a softer word. We like "service" now. We use the word such a lot, Christian service, but it is Christian slavery. Paul puts an emphasis on that: I'm a slave to Jesus; he has bought me; I belong to him; every part of my life belongs to him. What a statement, but the main thing is his calling. It is a double calling. His first calling is to be an apostle, and that simply means a sent one. I have been sent. When the Bible was translated from Greek into Latin, the word *apostello*, which means "I send", was changed to *mitto*, *mittere*. Same meaning, send, but it gradually became our word "missionary". Now "missionary" is no longer politically acceptable so may I suggest you use the word "missile"? It is the same word. A missionary is an intercontinental ballistic missile. That is how I like to talk. They have been sent; they have been missiled to another country to spread the gospel.

All these words mean the same thing: *sent*. Jesus was the chief apostle because Father sent him. He said, "As the Father sent me, so I send you," and a slave of Jesus will be sent somewhere to do something. That is part of being a slave, that you are sent. He then goes on to say that he was sent to spread the gospel. That is why he was a sent one, and the gospel was very clearly stated. He said it was promised in the Old Testament, and it centres on a person who is totally human and totally divine. The humanity comes from his birth and his incarnation, and his deity is declared in his resurrection.

Do you realise that it is the resurrection that is the heart of the gospel? Unfortunately, the Western churches have always made the death of Christ the focus of the gospel. Go into Eastern churches, especially the Eastern Orthodox ones, and you won't see a dead Christ. You won't see a crucifix. You will see pictures of a risen, ascending Christ looking at you – icons, they call them. The big difference between the Western churches, Catholic and Protestant, and the Eastern churches was that in the West we put the cross at the centre.

Paul never said we preach Christ crucified, but that is a favourite text in the West. He actually said, "We preach

Christ and him *having been* crucified." It is the risen Christ we teach, who was crucified. Not the Christ on the cross, the Christ who is risen and ascended, but who was crucified. We see the Lamb standing as if it had been slain. How can something that has been slain stand? The standing Christ in heaven was slain. That is getting the balance right.

It is the resurrection which God did. Jesus didn't rise, he *was raised* by God. This reversed the verdict that put him to death. It was God's last word on his Son's crucifixion: You were wrong, I bring my Son back to life to declare that he is my Son. It is the resurrection that proves Jesus was who he said he was. That is why a resurrection-centred gospel is better than a cross-centred gospel. So, Son of David by human descent; by incarnation, totally human; Son of God by divine declaration in the resurrection: he is my Son, and you have put him to death in the greatest injustice in history. The resurrection is God doing something and reversing the verdict that was passed on his Son. Then why didn't he stop it before the crucifixion? Because he sent him to be crucified, and that had to do something that could not be done any other way. We will come to that in chapter 3 of the epistle.

So here is the call of God, which made Paul the apostle take the gospel around the world, but who to take it to? Now we come to the amazing truth—that the most Jewish Jew God could have chosen was sent to the Gentiles. It is so typical of the Lord to send the very worst person to do something for him, or the most unsuitable. Here was a Hebrew of the Hebrews, descended from the tribe of Benjamin, a very exclusive little tribe, and even at his conversion God told him, "The Lord sent you to be an apostle to the Gentiles." Gentiles were people that Saul of Tarsus would not have touched. As a Pharisee he hated them, unclean people. Yet God said: this is your apostleship. God said, "You're to go to the Gentiles," and he is to go to all the Gentiles in the world. That is a big calling. In fact, that was his ambition for the then known world. He says, "I'm an apostle called to all the Gentiles and you, too." We can guess from this that the whole letter is really addressed to the Gentile believers in Rome, and he is going to talk to them about the Jews, whom they ought to be welcoming with a holy kiss instead of saying "God is finished with you". I find that particularly in Britain, churches are preaching that God is finished with the Jews. Someone needs to go and tell them, go and kiss the nearest Jew. A holy kiss, yes, but kiss them!

That is the drama behind this letter, and it is an amazing situation. Paul calls the Christians in Rome two things. He says, "You are beloved by God as sons," and, "You are belonging to God as saints." Here are Gentiles brought up in a Gentile, evil, wicked world, and yet Paul is saying: you are sons of God, and you are saints.

One of the things the Roman Catholic Church has got wrong is to have a few people called saint who get "canonised" (that doesn't mean shot at, it means shot up). In God's sight, as soon as you become a believer you are a saint . Whether you live up to that or not is another question. Try telling yourself every morning as you look in the mirror, "That is Saint ... there." Unfortunately, our translators of the Bible did not get the point. They have inserted two little words that should not be there. It says "called to be saints", but "to be" is not there in the Greek. It should not be there in the English either, but rendered "called saints". God called you a saint as soon as you belonged to him.

It reminds me of a mother who was having a baby baptised in a Methodist church in London. The minister said, "What do you want me to call this baby?"

She replied, "Genius."

"I beg your pardon – what?"

She repeated her request, "Call him Genius."

The minister said, "That's going to be a handicap all his life. Why do you want me to call him Genius?"

"I want to give him something to live up to," she affirmed.

That is logical. We are called saints because God has given us a title to live up to. The first meaning of the word "saint" is not a very holy person but someone set apart for God. A saint is someone who has been set apart from other people, set apart from other careers, set apart from a whole lot of things because they are set apart for God. The other part of the meaning of the word is that you are no use to God until you live up to that title. You have got a title, that is your status, how God sees you. You are one of the saints, and every believer in Jesus in Rome is addressed: the saints in Rome. Keep in mind that God calls us but cannot really use us until we begin to live up to our name, our title. Every Christian is a saint and should be living up to that.

So we have seen the description of Paul's *mission*. Now we turn to his *motivation*. The personal pronoun changes from "you" and "they" and "we"; it changes to "I". He makes a number of basic statements beginning with "I": "I remember you"; "I long to see you"; "I am bound"; "I am not ashamed" – and with each of these statements we get a little glimpse into Paul's heart, and his heart for the Gentiles to whom he wrote. Let us look at the four things that are revealed: his *intercession*, his *ambition*, his *obligation*, and his *satisfaction*. Take the first – his intercession. He says, "I remember you in my prayers." Now this tells us an amazing thing about Paul and that is, first, that he prays for churches that are not his, churches that he has not founded, churches he has never been to. He remembers and prays for them. We can get so obsessed with our own church and the church we have built that we forget other churches.

The most dramatic example of that in the church of which I was pastor was the day when we had our monthly business meeting, when we tried to do business the Lord's way. We asked the Lord to tell us what to do next, and a little old lady got up in one of our church meetings and said, "The Lord says, 'Finance the other churches in the town.'" A shock wave went through the church members. We had a big budget. We gave a third of it away to the poor, to missionaries. We supported all kinds of good causes, but we never gave any money to other churches in town. Have you ever heard of such a thing? This little old lady brought this word of prophecy.

We thought, "What do we have to do now?" I went to our bank manager, whose name was Julius Caesar. I am telling you the truth! Julius Caesar said to me, "What can I do for you?" I said, "We want to open a new account," and he said, "What for?" I said, "For the other churches in town," and he stared at me.

He said, "Dave, do you mean that?"

"Yes, the Lord told us that so we're going to do it."

We opened this new account, and it built up and up until there was a substantial balance in it. We did not know what to do with it. How do you go to another church and say, "We'll finance you"? Patronising! "Oh, you're showing off your riches now aren't you?" You know the kind of thing.

Then a tornado hit the town in which we lived and it took the roof right off a new Roman Catholic Church. We said, "Lord, you don't mean that Baptist money has to put the Catholic roof back on?" I went to the rather fat Irish priest and I gave him a huge cheque, and I said, "That's to put your roof back on." Well, if he had had a weak heart he would have been a goner!

He staggered back and said, "I never heard of a Baptist church financing a Roman Catholic Church."

"Well," I said, "There's a first for everything, and the Lord told us to do this."

He said, "You're the Bible church, aren't you?"

I was rather pleased that he said that, but it was easily understood because just a week or two earlier we had read the Bible right through, non-stop, from Sunday night to breakfast on Thursday morning. It takes eighty-four hours if you do it. Each person had read for fifteen minutes and passed the Bible on to someone else. We read round the clock, morning, noon and night. We had done this but we didn't know what would happen. Two thousand people came. We had lives changed, one after another. There is not space here to get into the stories of those lives, but we had no idea what we were doing when we planned it.

That had happened two or three weeks before this Catholic priest said, "You're the Bible church, aren't you?"

I said, "Yes, we'd like to be," and he said, "My people don't read the Bible. To tell you the truth, I don't. I give them a little homily every Sunday, but we don't do much with the Bible." Then he looked at me and said, "Would some of your people come to my people and teach us the Bible?" We carefully chose a very tactful team who went up there and taught that church the Bible.

It had all started with a little old lady in the church meeting saying, "We're going to finance other churches in town." When you listen to the Lord, doing the business his way, you have some big surprises, but they are lovely ones.

Paul prayed for other churches that he had not founded, that he had never visited. His prayer took two parts: thanksgiving and petition, or in simple language, "thank you" and "please" – two of six vital parts of prayer. He said, "I thank God for the reports that are spreading through the empire about your faith. You are becoming famous for your faith, and I thank God!" What a reputation for a church to have! Is rumour spreading about your church and about the faith? Thank God if it is. Then he said, "I ask, God, please let me go and see what I've heard." That was his petition. Whenever he thanked God for them he said, "Please God, can I go and see it for myself?" That's an understandable thing. It was not that he doubted, he just wanted to be encouraged and go and see it. That lies behind the phrase, "I remember you."

The next phrase reveals his *ambition*. He said, "My ambition is to come to you and do two things: to impart some spiritual gifts to you that will encourage you, [that's the believers], and I want to have a harvest among you." Paul was basically an evangelist and he wanted to come and bring some souls into the church. Here is the double ambition: *impart spiritual gifts* to the believers and *have a harvest* among the unbelievers. What an ambition!

Then he goes on to his *obligation*, and he says, "I am bound." Strong language – what did he feel bound to do? He is using slave language again. Many slaves were literally bound or chained, but he said, "I'm bound" – to do what? Well, to preach the gospel to the Greeks and the non-Greeks, the wise and the foolish. They are strange categories when you understand that the Roman Empire and its culture had come from Greece. Their organisation was Roman and their power was Roman, but their culture was Greek. Their education was Greek. The word "Greek" virtually means educated, cultured, and the non-Greek meant not educated, not cultured. In Rome you had both, side by side. Paul's gospel was for both. It was not just for educated people, it was for the uneducated. It was not just for the social snobs at one end. It was for everybody, and so he says "I'm bound" – to Greeks and non-Greeks, and that explains why he wanted to come really. It is the heart of an evangelist. The Romans had conquered Greece, but in culture the Greeks had conquered Romans.

We come to his final statement, which is exciting. "I am not ashamed of the gospel!" Now that is such an emphatic statement that I believe he must have been tempted to be ashamed. Little did he realise that when he finally came to Rome he would be chained to a Roman soldier. How humiliating to arrive in the capital of the empire in chains. That is God's way, isn't it? So unexpected!

Why is Paul not ashamed? Because it is *power*. A friend of mine was going to a communist country and he was stopped at the customs. The customs officer said, "What's in that case?"

He replied, "Dynamite."

I am afraid it delayed his entry into the country, but when they opened the case it was full of gospel tracts. They said, "Why did you call this dynamite?"

He said, "Because it *is* dynamite."

The actual Greek word here is *dunamis*. "I'm not ashamed of the gospel because it's power" – and he knew the Roman Empire worshipped power. They were built on their own power, but he is saying: I've got a power bigger than the power of the Roman Empire.

Again he was not to know that within three hundred years the Emperor would be claiming to be a Christian. He was not to know that they would turn the world upside-down. Actually, they were turning it right way up, but when you live upside-down you think it is being turned upside-down. Do you follow me? We are those who turn the world right-way up. Keep emphasising that. The power of God to do *what*? The power of God to *save*, to *salvation*. That is a word we do not really use much now in normal life. I go back to the World War II days, and I remember how we had a word that was on everybody's lips: *salvage*. We salvaged everything for the war effort. We salvaged paper, metal, old cooking pans – and we used salvaged materials to build Spitfires. The word now is recycle. It is not a bad equivalent for "salvation". God has power to recycle men and women.

It is a good word because hell is God's rubbish dump. It is where useless people are thrown. God does not *send* people to hell, he *throws* them there. That is the verb he used all the time. You don't place rubbish in a bin, you throw it away. You throw it in the bin. Hell, God's rubbish dump, is where he throws people who have perished like a rubber hot water bottle that has perished. It looks like a bottle, but it is no use for the purpose for which it was made. The tragedy of not being saved is to become no use to God and to be thrown away into the fire. That is hell. *The gospel is to salvage men and women from that.*

I was invited to preach at the annual lawyer's service in a church called the Temple in the Strand in London. Once a year all the judges and lawyers and solicitors come together and fill the church, and they invite someone to come and preach to them. I didn't know what I was going to say, and then I thought of a phrase in Romans that I would use. I gave out my text. It was a fearsome occasion. The pulpit was like a dock in a court, and I felt I was on trial. The big judges were all sitting in a row. They didn't have wigs on, but they looked just as impressive. Here was I on trial in this pulpit and I said, "My text is 'What the law could not do, God did.'" I told them the law may punish a man for being bad, the law may prevent others from committing the same crime by fear, but the one thing the law cannot do is turn a bad man into a good man. It just can't do it. You might persuade him to try.

I continued, "I know a man who belonged to the worst gang in East London." (He was a member of the Kray brothers' gang, the man who got rid of the bodies for them.) A Greek, he was called Chris Lambrianou. Chris was in solitary confinement for fifteen years, and he was suicidal. They had cemented his iron bedstead to the floor of the cell. One day somebody gave him a box of books to read, and in it was a Bible. He thought, "I've heard of this book – supposed to do you a lot of good. I'll try sleeping on it," and he put it under his pillow. For the first time in years, he slept. He thought, "This is a good book. I'll wear it inside my shirt," and from then on he wore it next to his heart, and he felt better and better and better. Finally he decided to try to read it. So, it having done so much good to him, he started reading it. One night in his solitary cell he was woken up with a start in the middle of the night, and there were three bearded men standing at the foot of his bunk. He said, "I know who you are. You're the Father, you're the Son, and you're the Spirit." The middle one said, "Just follow me," and from that moment Chris was a new man. He became soft and gentle, and this man who had spent his days getting rid of bodies was going to court to save young men from prison. The judge of the local court from then on sentenced young men who were in trouble to living a year with Chris. "I sentence you to go and live with that man for one year." He spends his year making bad youths into good youths. That's the power of God – salvaging people, recycling them; saving them from rubbish, from perishing, from becoming useless. I get excited about this!

Says Paul, "This must be first for the Jew and then for the Gentile." That should be a Christian's missionary strategy: first for the Jew, then for the Gentile. If there are any Jews near where you live, God is saying, "Go to them first." It is what Paul always did in every city. He went to the Jew first, and if they refused, he turned to the Gentile. The church has got a long way away from that priority. It was, after all, God's strategy for the whole world. In the Old Testament God started with the Jew first, and said, "Now you're to be a light to the Gentiles." Adopt God's strategy: to the Jew first and then the Gentile. That was the power of God. That does not mean that God prefers Jews. He has no favourites, but that is his order of working. It always has been, it always will be, and yet the Gentile church seems to have forgotten that altogether.

Finally, *righteousness from God*. The power of God to salvation, to salvage, to recycle, and the righteousness from God. It is all in that little word *from*. Martin Luther was scared of the righteousness of God. It was a threat. It meant judgment. A righteous God has to judge. A righteous God has to punish. A righteous God has to send people to hell. A righteousness *of* God is not good news but righteousness *from* God is. It is God saying, "I know you're not righteous. I know what you've done." To me he said, "I know the worst about you" – but the gospel is: *you can have righteousness from God*. He can share his righteousness with you because it comes by faith. From beginning to end, it is faith. It is from faith, to faith. You don't ever get past faith. *You go on believing, and those who will be saved are those who go on believing to the end*. We will come back to that thought.

Finally, Paul, a good Jew, quotes scripture. Scripture has the last word. It is the final authority for any Jew, and he quotes Habakkuk, one of my favourite prophets of the Old Testament. Habakkuk was the man who argued with God and lost the argument, as you always will, but God loves people who argue with him. Habakkuk argued with God and said, first, "God, what are you doing about the state of Jerusalem? It's dreadful and you're sitting up there in heaven doing nothing! Why don't you do something?"

God said, "But I am doing something, Habakkuk."

"What are you doing?"

"Well, I'm bringing the Babylonians."

Now Habakkuk was so shocked with that he said, "God, you couldn't do that. They believe in a scorched earth policy. They not only kill all the people; they kill all the animals; they kill all the trees and cut them down. There isn't a tree left standing when the Babylonians come. You will kill the few good people in Jerusalem along with all the bad ones. You are of purer eyes than to behold iniquity."

That is not God's statement. That is Habakkuk arguing with God – "You couldn't do that."

God said, "I could and I will."

Habakkuk finally got through all that to a real act of faith where he started singing a lovely song which I have set to music and in chapter 3 of Habakkuk he says, "Though the trees are cut down, no tree is budding and there's no fruit on the fig tree, yet I will rejoice in God my Saviour."

Because God said to Habakkuk, "You think I will allow the Babylonians to destroy the righteous along with the wicked? No, the righteous, the just, will survive by keeping faith." That is the real meaning of the verse. I am afraid Luther did not quite get the real meaning. The real meaning is: *Don't worry when my judgment comes. The righteous will survive by keeping faith with me.* That, of course, is true for all of us. When the final judgment of God comes, the righteous will live by faith. We shall survive by keeping faith with God.

2. SIN AND WRATH

ROMANS 1:18–3:20

A. GENTILES – "They" (1:18-32)
    1. Idolatry – people gave God up (18-23)
        a. Suppression of truth (18-20)
        b. Substitution of lies (21-23)
    2. Immorality – God gave up people (14-32)
        a. Depraved bodies (24-27)
        b. Debased minds (28-32)

B. JEWS – "you" (2:1-29)
    1. Secrecy (1-5)
        a. Condemnation of others
        b. Contempt for God
    2. Shame (6-16)
        a. Conduct
        b. Conscience
    3. Superiority (17-29)
        a. Commandments
        b. Circumcision

C. JEW AND GENTILE – "we" (3:1-20)
    1. Jewish defence (1-8)
        a. First advantage – divine word
        b. First arguments – human word
    2. Human depravity (9-20)
        a. Survey in scripture
        b. Silence before law

PLEASE READ ROMANS 1:18–3:20

The most important thing about this study is that *the gospel is bad news before it can be good news*. In other words, you have got to talk about sin and the wrath of God if you are going to understand the gospel. I remember when I bought an engagement ring for my wife. We went into a jeweller's shop and asked to see some rings. First of all, he carefully covered the counter with black velvet cloth and then he brought out the rings to show us. You could only see the beauty of the ring against the black cloth. You can only understand the gospel as good news if you realise the bad news. The bad news is quite simply what people need to be saved from. It is no use talking about salvation if we don't tell people what they need to be saved from.

When I am counselling a new enquirer, I always get around to one particular question. I ask them, "You want to be a Christian?"

"Yes."

"Do you want to accept Jesus as your Saviour and Lord?"

"Yes."

"What sins do you want him to save you from?"

That is the key question. Repentance only begins at that point. They always say, "All of them," to which I reply, "You haven't committed all of them. What sins do you want him to save you from?" It is only then that they begin to name them and be specific about sins. Christ did not come to save us from hell. That is a bonus thrown in. His name means he came to save his people from their sins – all of them. Until you are saved from all of them you are not saved yet.

I had better tell you straightaway I'm not saved yet, but I am on "the way" of salvation. I am looking forward to being

41

saved, aren't you? Paul is going to say in Romans 13, "We are nearer our salvation than when we first believed." I have never heard that preached on – of salvation as future, as well as past. We are looking forward to being saved. I am looking forward to the day when there is no trace of sin left in me, when I am perfectly restored to the image of God. That is when I shall be saved, and then and only then will I shout, "Once saved, always saved," because then it will be true.

Now all this is due to the fact that the word "sin" has dropped out of use. Again, it is not politically correct, but we have got to face the darkness of sin and what it is like and what it means quite specifically. Only then will we understand the gospel. Only then will we appreciate it. Until you understand the wrath of God you will not appreciate the love of God. It is as simple as that. Paul said, "I'm not ashamed of the gospel," and this is where it begins. The wrath of God is being revealed from heaven. That is the first part of revelation – the wrath, the anger of God. People have tried to explain it away as his holy indignation, but it is more than that. God hates sin. It has ruined his Creation, for us as well as for him. God hates it, and until we realise that God hates sin, we will not really appreciate that God loves sinners.

This is very important, so we start with wrath before love. The God of the Bible has two sides to his character. On the one hand, he loves people. On the other hand, he hates people. On the one hand, he punishes people. On the other hand, he pardons people. On the one hand, he shows his justice; on the other hand, his mercy. If we forget either of those two sides we will preach a distorted gospel. The first thing we have to consider in this passage is the wrath of God being revealed, first against Gentiles, then against Jews, then against everybody, for, as it will be summed up, we have all sinned. Jesus said this: "When the Holy

Spirit has come to you, he will convict the world of three things: sin, righteousness and judgment. A person needs to understand all those three words if they are going to make any headway in the Christian life – the fact of sin, the fact of righteousness, and the fact of judgment when the two meet. The righteousness of God is a threat. The righteousness from God is an offer. It is keeping those two things together that we are concerned about now.

Beginning with the Gentiles, Paul talks about them in the third person – "they", talking about the Gentile, Roman world in which these people were brought up. He is tactful, assuming they have all left it behind. What is it in this godless world? The first fact is that people give God up. Once they have done that, God responds quite positively by giving them up. That is only fair and just. If we give him up, he gives us up. Look at both sides of this. First of all, people give God up, and of course, whenever the Bible talks about God it is not about any "god". It is not talking about other religions, it is about the God of Israel, who is the only one who really exists. No other God exists. They are all figments of the imagination. That is part of the Christian truth, but it is very offensive in a world that is wanting to bring all religions together.

Tony Blair, our former Prime Minister, is now building up a huge foundation of his own to bring all religions together from around the world. Of course this was behind Shimon Peres of Israel going to the Pope and suggesting the same thing. It is becoming the most popular idea in the world – that we bring all religions into one. The Bible does predict that there will be one world religion one day, but it is not going to be a religion of God. It will be a religion of the Antichrist, not of Christ, but that is the talk today. Now Paul accuses godless people of doing two things: suppressing the truth about God and substituting lies. One is a positive, the other a negative accusation. They are suppressing the truth. Now that is quite an insight into human nature. As Paul goes on to point out, there is no excuse for atheism. There is no excuse for not believing in God because everybody has access to the truth about God in two ways: one, creation around us; and, two, conscience within us.

Creation around us should tell us that God is powerful and divine, that the person who put all this in space and brought it all into being must be a powerful God. His power and his divinity I have called his 'Godness'. We must not think of God as a big human being; God is God. There is only one God and there is no one else like him. His 'Godness' is clearly seen in what he has made. You just need to go and study the trees around us and you should know that God is an amazing God. God is a creative God. There are no two blades of grass the same, no two snowflakes the same, no two clouds the same. What an amazing, creative artist he is! There are no two people the same. Even identical twins have their differences. What a God! It is visible in everything his hand has made, so we are without excuse.

When the Bible refers to atheism it does not mean someone who does not believe in God but someone who ignores God, someone for whom God is not part of their life, someone who can go right through life without thinking about God at all. That is a deliberate suppression of truth. They could have known, and they have suppressed that knowledge. How often I have found that when trying to reach an unconverted person! You find they are deliberately suppressing. If you answer one question satisfactorily they will come up with another one. Answer that and they will come up with another one, and you finally come to the conclusion they do not want to know the truth. They are suppressing it. Why? Because they would have to change.

Take the resurrection. The evidence for it would convince

any jury on earth that Jesus rose from the dead. That is why so many top lawyers have become Christians. There are more Christians in the legal profession than in any other. If they are prepared to examine the evidence, they are convinced that Jesus rose from the dead. I could give you a list of the most prominent lawyers in Britain who, after examining the evidence for the resurrection, have had to change their minds, but they have had to change their lives too. That is why most people won't face the evidence, because if Jesus did rise from the dead then everything he said is also true. That means my life has to change from a self-centred life to a God-centred life, and not many people want that. So people suppress the truth. They suppress the evidence.

There is plenty of evidence outside the Bible for the existence of Jesus and for his miracles – historical records that are not in our Bible which say he was a wonder worker. People do not want to know about that evidence even if you produce it. There is that within godlessness which says, "I don't want to know! I've never believed in God, and I don't intend to now." That is suppression of truth. Every living being has access to the creation outside us and the conscience within us and should know that there is a God and that right and wrong matter to him, and that we are made in his image and therefore have that sense of right and wrong. Even the most primitive savage on earth has a conscience and will tell you what is right and wrong. Mind you, we usually see what is wrong in other people more easily than we see it in ourselves, but we know the difference and we say, "That's wrong! He or she shouldn't be doing that." That is God giving us the same sense of right and wrong as he has.

Not only do godless people suppress the truth, they have to substitute lies for the truth. That is because there is a God-shaped blank in every human being that has to be filled with something or someone to worship. I don't need to tell you of the young people today who worship pop stars. You can see them with arms upraised and clapping and doing everything else and worshipping someone of their own kind. They have substituted a creature for the Creator. If you watch grown men at a football match, football is the religion of England for many men. They get very religious at a football match and fling themselves around and shout and cheer. You can't imagine any of them going to church and doing the same thing, but they are worshipping a bunch of men and a lump of leather on the pitch. They will talk about that team as if they are talking about a god with whom they identify and whom they worship on Saturday afternoons. You see, we cannot be godless people without substituting something or someone into that God-shaped blank in our human soul.

There is therefore, as Paul says, no excuse whatever. People are exchanging darkness for light. They are exchanging mortals for immortal, and it is a substitute religion. Of course, religion itself, being religious, can become a substitute for God. Probably the majority of the human race wants to be religious in one way or another, and therefore they imagine their God. In Britain itself I know just how many people tell me, "Well, this is what I think God is like..." and it is not what the Bible reveals he said about himself, it is what they think God is like. They have built an image of God in their minds and it is pure imagination, but it is the God they like to think of, the God they even pray to.

A student came up to a friend of mine and said, "I've been looking for God so long, and I can't find him." My friend said to him, "Well, how strange! He's been looking for you for longer than that. However have you missed each other then?" That was a pretty good answer because the God that the student was looking for was the God of his own imagination, the God he wanted to find. The God he believed in was not the God who showed himself to be the God of Israel. That is of great offence to the world that the only God there exists is the God of Israel. The philosophers call that the "scandal of particularity". Let me tell you what that means. It is a scandal that God should speak to only one nation on earth. Why didn't God speak to the Americans or the Russians or the Australians or the British? Why did God have to reveal himself to the Jews and tell them to tell everybody else? Philosophers cannot accept that scandal of particularity, but it is the way God has chosen to reveal himself.

We had three children. One is now in heaven, but the other two are still with us on earth. When our three children were little I brought them sweets (or candies) every Saturday. I had a choice. I could either give one of them a bag of sweets and say, "Share that with your brother and sister," or I could say, "I've got three bars of chocolate, one for you and one for you and one for you." Now if I gave them in the second way we had peace, but if I gave them in the first way we didn't. "You've got more than I have!" There was argument and dissension because I gave to one child to share with the others. That is God's method. He said, "I'm going to give you, Abraham, everything I can, and your descendants, and you will bless all the families of the earth."

Now that is a scandal. It means the world, if it is going to find God, has to go to the Jews to find him and particularly to the Jew Jesus, to find him, and that is offensive. "Why should I have to go to the Jews?" One British poet wrote a very simple, short poem which goes like this: "How odd of God to choose the Jews." Another poet added an extra verse: "But odder still are those who choose the Jewish God and scorn the Jews." Those two English poets had summed it all up. We are all indebted to the Jews. The Bible I teach is a Jewish book through and through. The Jesus who saved you is a Jew. The apostles were all Jewish. The church was solidly Jewish at the beginning and will catch up in the end, too.

I once said to a Jew in a shop I was visiting, "My best friend is a Jew." He looked quite pleased about that. I said, "In fact, he saved my life." He looked really doubly pleased. He was almost puffing out with pride, and he said, "Who was that?" That was when it all collapsed, but it is true. I am going to jump ahead and say we are to make Jews jealous, not envious. Most people don't know the difference. The NIV got it wrong, and in chapter 11 it says we are to make the Jews envious. No, make them jealous. How do you do that? Not by talking about what we have found but about what we have found of *theirs*. We have found their Messiah. We are reading their Bible. We have found their Jesus. We worship their God, and we do that gladly because we believe they have the truth and that their God is the only one who exists. We will see more of that in Romans 11 and I am jumping ahead.

So here is this terrible accusation of the Gentiles that they have suppressed the truth and substituted lies and have become foolish though they think they are wise. They are self-deluded. That is a very dangerous form of deception. Idolatry is giving God up and producing something or someone else to take his place. What does that lead to? God giving them up, and we now see the signs of God's wrath in society. They are listed here and it reads like a police station desk blotter or a cheap Sunday newspaper. It is an amazing description of what happens when you give God up. The answer is he doesn't just remain aloof and indifferent, he acts – he shows his anger.

Now there are two words for the anger of God in the Greek language, and it is interesting how both are used in the New Testament. One is for simmering anger and the other is for anger that boils over. If I can use a simple illustration: if you put a pan of milk on the stove to warm for a drink, you are very foolish if you don't watch it carefully because it will begin to simmer and little bubbles will come to the surface. If you ignore that, it will come to the point where it suddenly boils over, makes a mess, it gets burnt and you have a mess on your hands to clear up. God's anger is a bit like that. At the moment, God's anger is simmering, and unless you watch carefully you will miss the bubbles coming up. One day it is going to boil over, and that is called the day of wrath in Romans 2. God's wrath is revealed in two phases. In phase one it is simmering and not too obvious except to those who are watching and who recognise what is happening. On the day of wrath, God's anger will boil over, and that is a day when he will really deal with all those who have spoiled his world.

Paul writes about God's amazing patience and tolerance in waiting before it boils over. First we look at God's anger just bubbling up to the surface. I see it very clearly in England and indeed throughout the Western world and other countries influenced by the West. God's anger is really simmering. The little bubbles that come up are described here. They are described first in terms of bodies and then in terms of minds. When God gives human beings up, something happens to their bodies and to their minds. All of that is God's bubbling wrath just under the surface. It is getting hotter.

Let us consider debased bodies and depraved minds, because that is what the Bible talks about. When God gives men up he is giving them up to themselves, to all that is bad in themselves. Now most if not all of us have homosexuality in our bodies. It may come out in a harmless way when we are in our teens and we get a crush for a teacher or an adult person of the same sex, but we are all capable of homosexuality because that is in us all. When God gives you up he takes the brakes off, and he leaves you up to what he calls your shameful desires. When God does not hold on to you, what you really want to do comes out, and it is not very nice. One thing that is clearly described here is that you have become anti-sexual. That is what happens to your body. What happens to your mind is that it becomes antisocial.

When you read through the list in Romans 1 you are reading what is happening all around us. God made male and female. He made us that way for each other and for marriage between one man and one woman. That is God's plan for sex – sex within marriage and commitment, and not sex outside that. That was God's plan, but as soon as he gives people up they become antisexual. One of the first things that happen is that men begin to have sex with men and women with women, which God never intended, never planned. It is within us all, so don't condemn people and say, "You're a homosexual." Say to yourself, "I could be there if God didn't keep his hand on me." I think that is nearer the truth. Then you begin to understand what is happening around you.

We have now passed laws in England for same-sex marriage, and it is now officially possible for a man to marry a man and a woman to marry a woman. That is anti-sexual rebellion against God. It is distorting his order for family and for happiness, but we have fallen for it and it is going to spread around the whole world, believe it or not. It will come, mark my words, because godless people do not like God's way of living. That is within all of us. We have a fallen nature with wrong desires. It is not just in the realm of sex, it is in the realm of food. You can eat to live or live to eat. That is another of our shameful desires. God created food for us to enjoy, to live, but we have turned it into a little god. Our television programmes in Britain are now packed with gourmet programmes as to how to make more exciting food and tickle your fancy. People are swallowing it all as if they're living for food rather than eating to live.

It can happen with money. Money is a very good servant but a horrible master. You can use it for good purposes, but if you once devote yourself to money as a god you are worshipping mammon, and you have become addicted. Businessmen who have made all that they could possibly need for the rest of their lives will go on grabbing new businesses, grabbing more money because they will never be satisfied. Addictions cannot be satisfied. They act like drugs, and you need more and more and more to satisfy. I think you can see in all this that we are talking about the real world in which we live. We are talking about what is happening around us, and that is the wrath of God being revealed, which is turning good desires into addictions. It is not just young people. I see it in every age group. You can see God giving men up because they have given him up and think they can get away with it.

I was speaking in a factory canteen once, and a man got up and said, "What do you think of this? I'm not boasting, but I live a good life. All the other workers around me will tell you how helpful I am to them. My neighbours at home in the street will tell you that if they are ever in trouble I'm the one they turn to. I'm the one that helps them. But I don't pray; I don't go to church; I don't read the Bible. How do you explain that?"

I just looked him in the face and I said, "You don't go to church; you don't pray; you don't read the Bible, but I'll bet your grandfather did," and he collapsed. He did not realise that you can be living on your parents' and grandparents' faith up to about the third or fourth generation, but if you kill the root of Christianity you will then lose the fruit. You are seeing it happen all around us. People said in my day, "Why be married in church?" Now they say, "Why be married at all?"

It happens over two or three generations very clearly. You lose your spiritual capital and the result is that your grandchildren or great-grandchildren have not inherited the root and cannot maintain the fruit. Again, that is happening on a wide scale. You can see God's wrath in it all and, in a sense, God's mercy. He is showing us where this all leads. He is saying: You're on a wrong course, and you can now see it because I'm helping you to see it. I'm giving people up to themselves.

It is not just food, fame, control, money, possessions. You can see that happening all around you, but it is what is happening to minds too, not just anti-sexual bodies or bodies given over to shameful desires. I don't think sex is a shameful desire. If it is used God's way it is a pleasure, but if not used God's way it becomes an addiction and a shameful desire.

Now let us look at what happens to the mind. When you read the list in Romans 1, you are reading of minds that are antisocial, rebellious to parents, gossips. There is a whole long list of things that the mind has been filled with and that explain antisocial behaviour.

First, *wickedness*. That means, simply, a general attitude of unrightness, injustice – of unrighteousness, as the Bible would put it. In other words, a liking for the wrong thing. (Have you noticed how children learn the word "no" before the word "yes"?)

Then *evil*, meaning a desire to do harm, to injure other people, to drag them down with you. The title the Bible gives to the devil is "the evil one". "Lead us not into temptation, but deliver us from the evil one...." is the Lord's Prayer.

Covetousness—the word in the Greek means, literally, to want more. Is there no trace of that in your heart and mind? Have you never wanted more than you have? Have you never been discontent with your lot?

Malice means viciousness; wanting to attack people.

Envy is next, a warped and twisted emotion responsible for the first murder in history and the worst murder in history. Pilate knew that for envy they had delivered Jesus up, and

Cain killed Abel for envy; and envy gets right into hearts of Christian workers. Preachers have been envious of another preacher's gift. Sunday school teachers have been envious of a Sunday school teacher who does it better than they do. Christian singers have been envious of another singer's voice. Members of a church are envious that somebody else was elected to the diaconate and not them. Is there no trace of envy in your mind?

Murder – you might say, "Well, I'm quite sure I would never murder someone." Just a minute! Jesus said that if ever you have been angry with someone, or if ever you have despised them and called them a fool, you are a murderer in thought. Murder is there in your mind.

Strife means contending because of pride and ambition; as somebody crudely put it, wanting to stand on the faces of those below you and lick the boots of those above you; to argue; to push yourself up to the top. No trace of that?

Deceit means crafty cunning. There can be ulterior motives; underhand methods. We've got nothing of that in our mind?

Malignity means, putting the worst construction on the things that you hear; interpreting them wrongly with a view to painting a worse picture than is actually true.

Gossips – the word literally means whisperers; people who whisper about others behind their backs; members in a church who speak about the business outside the church meeting and not inside it.

Slanderers are those who openly speak about others and destroy their reputation.

Haters of God means those who don't like the idea of God because he puts brakes on you; because he says, "Thou shalt not..."; because he limits your activity.

Insolent means defiant; rude to those who are superior to you.

Haughty means proud; it has been called the summit of all the sins.

Boastful means pretending to be or to have or to do what in fact you are not, and have not, and do not.

Inventors of evil means those who are constantly finding new ways of sinning.

Disobedient to parents could mean a teenager who says, "Who made you an authority over me?"; a young person who ignores the wisdom and experience of parents.

Foolish means utterly unreasonable; unapproachable; can't be talked to.

Faithless means a man who breaks his promises; when he's made a promise, signed an agreement, he doesn't keep it. He says, "Yes, I'll turn up and give out hymn books at six o'clock for the service," and doesn't turn up till twenty past. This is what this word refers to.

Heartless means to be without natural affection; to have an inability to make friends.

Ruthless means to be cruel and pitiless to other people.

Is there a single person who could stand up and say, "There's nothing of that in my mind"? If there's anything of any of these things in your mind, do you realise that if God takes the brakes off that's what you will become? That will be the mind that will operate, that will be your personality. Is there anyone who dares to say that this has nothing to say to us? By the grace of God, these things, which are in my mind, do not come out as they would if he took the brakes off, but when God gives men up, these are the things that appear.

So behaviour springs from our minds – how we think and what we are, and that again is God at work and showing us clearly where this is going to lead. I am pleased that some Christians in their own field are pointing out where this will lead and can see and now prove statistically the results in the next generation. That is good, and it is a good thing for us to do. It is part of exposing evil, but the world will not easily see it. They follow their addictions, and it is not easy to stop that.

So there are debased bodies and depraved minds, and one of the climaxes of a depraved mind is that not only are they constantly thinking of new ways to do bad things themselves, they positively encourage others to do the same, because if you are behaving in a wrong fashion, comfort can come by saying, "Well, others are doing it too." You become an evangelist for evil. That is the last verse in chapter 1 – "Not only do they do these things themselves, but they encourage and approve them in other people." It spreads like an infection. Addiction and infection go together. They spread alarmingly quickly, and that is Ebola in a spiritual sense. We are, after all, inherently self-centred people, and all God has to do to show his wrath to us is to let us go. If you have a car parked on a hill and you take the brake off, what is going to happen? It will just go downhill. If you wonder why society is heading the way it is, the simple explanation is God has taken the brake off. That is how his wrath shows at the moment. It is not boiling over. When it does, the world will really wake up and realise, but it is simmering. Those who watch and pray can see it, and can see it happening, and can warn people of what the results are.

So that is Gentiles and how they sin, and it is open, blatant, unembarrassed, unashamed. But when you turn to the Jews their sin is of a rather different kind. It is still sin, but first it is hidden. Moving to the Jewish sin, the pronoun changes from "they" to "you" and even "we" because Paul counts himself as a Jew. The first thing he says is: "You're hypocrites. You condemn it in others and you do it yourself." It is interesting that psychologists would tell us we are good at accusing others of the very things that are our weaknesses because we spot it. It takes one to know one. You point a finger at somebody else and you have three fingers pointing back at yourself. That is the moral of this passage. Condemnation of others comes happily to those who are hiding their own sins. That was the Pharisees to a tee in Jesus' day. That is why he called them whitewashed sepulchres (tombs). If the Gentiles display their sins and approve others, Jews tend to disapprove sin in others and hide it in themselves.

I remember a Jew in Jerusalem saying to me, "We Jews are just human, only more so." I thought that really summed it up. He said, "If people are greedy, we Jews can be as greedy as anyone else. If people are this, we can do it better." He was really telling me they can do virtue and vice better than anyone else, and they can. Jews have many good virtues. Family life is second to none, but their vices are equally more than human. It is part of God's calling to them that they are to be a demonstration to the world. If they don't choose to be the demonstration of his mercy, they will be a demonstration of his justice. That's the meaning of the potter and the clay.

I hope you understand why the Bible suggests we are clay in the potter's hands. It is not suggesting that God is responsible for everything in us. Jeremiah was taken (you can read it in chapter 18 of his book) to the potter's house, to watch the potter with a wheel. He is pedalling away with his feet, the wheel is spinning round, and he throws a lump of clay on the wheel. Jeremiah watched him try to make it into a beautiful vase, a lovely shape, but the clay would not run in his hands. So he took the same clay and put it back into a lump, threw in on the wheel and made a crude pot that would be used maybe in the kitchen for something. Jeremiah was asked by the Lord, who decided whether that clay became a beautiful vase or ugly pot, and had to say: "The clay; not the potter, the clay." Then the Lord said to Jeremiah, "I wanted to make Israel a beautiful nation for the world to see my righteousness, but they would not respond to my hand, and so I am going to make them an ugly pot of my justice." It underlines it was Israel's choice.

Every one of us is the vessel of God we have chosen to be. We either respond to God's touch and let his hands mould us into a beautiful man or woman, or else he will make us an ugly example of his justice. The choice will be ours, not his. He is the potter, and he will make us one thing or the other, but the choice will be ours. Do you understand now the picture of the potter and the clay? It Is not a helpless picture. We have a chorus, "You are the potter; I am the clay," as much to say, "I'm just clay in your hands." No, I can choose to let the Lord make me beautiful or make me ugly, but it will be my choice, not his. That is an amazing insight which helps us when we read Romans 9, which brings up again the potter and the clay picture.

Now those who condemn others are passing judgment on others and must face divine judgment because they do the same thing. To condemn others is to be in danger of being in contempt of God (see 2:1ff).

God's kindness, tolerance and patience puts up with an amazing lot from people. Why does God not destroy them straight away? I always smile when somebody says to me, "Why doesn't God destroy all the bad people in the world now? Then the rest of us could live in peace and harmony." Have you had someone say that to you? The fatal flaw in the argument is that they are always sure they would still be around. If God destroyed all those who are spoiling the world, I would not be teaching and you would not be sitting there reading this. If God had dealt with me in justice I would not be here.

Praise God for his kindness, his tolerance, his patience; but if I take advantage of that I am storing up wrath for the day of wrath. Nobody gets away with it. God keeps a record.

That is comforting when I read of young men bursting into old-age pensioners' cottages in England and raping them and getting away with it. Seventy-five percent of crime in Britain is not discovered. It pays to be a criminal now. You stand a better chance nowadays of getting away with it, but nobody gets away with it with God. You are storing up wrath for the day of wrath when it boils over. That is going to be an awful day.

That is part of the message of the book of Revelation, where even people suffering to the nth degree are stubbornly refusing to repent. "I'm not going to change, whatever God does." He is going to give an increasing exposure of his wrath to people as we near the end of history. That is the message of Revelation – not to those who trust him but to the world there are very rough days coming, which will demonstrate God's wrath and make it clearer and clearer that God is angry at the spoiling of his world. Still stubborn human beings will not repent (change their minds), so the divine restraint is taken off, but nevertheless he is still tolerant of so much. Human repentance is a difficult thing for anyone to do.

Now the next thing about the Jews and their sin is their shame compared with people who have never known better. It is an extraordinary comparison. They have had the law, and they know perfectly well that though we are justified by faith we are judged by works—everybody. That is an important double statement. We may be justified by faith, but we will all be judged by works, or by the little word "do". Here is a key word in this next section. It is the word: "We shall be judged by what we *do*," and I underline that it applies as much to Christians as to anybody else. In 2 Corinthians Paul says, "We [we believers] must all appear before the judgment seat of Christ to receive according to the things done in the body." That means done in this life. Judgment is always on deeds, what we have done, and therefore Paul dares to say that a person who has persistently done good will be accepted by God, and a person who has persistently done evil will be condemned. The key is the word "do". By comparison he says, to rebuke the Jew, there are Gentiles who do the right thing, and they have no law – they have never heard the Ten Commandments, but they have done the right thing. How come? He says that they have the law of God written in their hearts. There is the conscience again.

This is the answer to how will God judge those who have never heard the gospel, a frequently asked question. The answer is that God will judge everybody according to the light they have received – no more, no less. In other words, everyone will be judged by what they consider to be wrong in others. That is a thought. Whatever you consider wrong in others, God will hold against you if you are doing the same thing – another dig at the secrecy angle. Do you know that sin was in the world long before the Moses' law came in, long before the Ten Commandments? I have made a list of the things that humanity recognised as being wrong before Moses gave the laws. Here is the list: coveting, idolatry, murder, profligacy, adultery, pride, selfishness, dishonouring parents, injustice, incest – and almost every society on earth has said incest is wrong. They have not got that from the Bible. They have got it from the law of God written in their hearts – and deceit. Every one of those things is condemned as wrong in the book of Genesis before any law was given. Everybody knew. To shame the Jews, Paul is telling them: there are Gentiles who know enough to do some good things, and you have had so much more knowledge, you Jews. You should be that much better people.

In fact, the world expects that of Israel – have you noticed? The world will condemn Israel for things they do not condemn in anybody else. Why? It is because they expect the Jewish people, who have given the highest moral standards to the world, to live up to them. They judge Israel by a higher standard than any other nation because they have had more revelation, because they have given the Ten Commandments to the world. These are maybe new thoughts to you, but God is absolutely fair. He will never judge a person by light he did not receive. To every human being God will say: Whatever you see wrong, especially in other people, I will judge you by. He is absolutely fair; nothing could be more just.

We are still in the bad news, by the way. The next thing Paul mentions is the superiority of Jews, the fact that they have the commandments, whether they keep them or not. The fact that they gave the world the commandments gives Jews a sense of superiority. He is telling them this: you may have instructed others, but you did not bother to instruct yourself; you ignored yourself; you gave the world the commandments, and you do not keep them.

The other thing in 2:25–29 about which Jews are complacent and even boastful is that they have circumcision. There are just a few things that have enabled the Jews to keep their identity after being scattered among the nations for so many years. One is the Sabbath (they have kept the Sabbath wherever they have gone), another is the diet and the third is circumcision, that small removal of the foreskin of a man's penis that marks him out as a son of Abraham. Paul now says that circumcision that is only outward and physical will be quite irrelevant on the Day of Judgment. It matters nothing to God unless it is matched by a circumcision in the heart. When the desires of the flesh are removed from the heart, that circumcision really matters to God. So the Jews have their sense of superiority over the commandments, and over circumcision, but it is no use to them unless they keep them.

The next thing he condemns in Jewish sin is self-justification. This is very common among Jewish people and is taught to them. It was a Jew who came up to Jesus and was willing to justify himself." The one thing you can't ever do is justify yourself. You know what justify means, I'm sure. If a man comes home very late, early hours of the morning, half drunk, the wife will say, "Justify yourself. Explain it to me. Prove to me that you were in the right." That's what they mean. Self-justification is very common. How did the Jews do that? Well, first on the grounds that they brought the revelation of God to the world. They can justify their sin by pointing that out. The revelation they were entrusted with, God's Word, and only they gave the world God's Word. They can feel complacent about that. That justifies however they behave, but Paul says, "Look, even if all of you were not believing, were faithless to God, God's word is still faithful. Let every man be a liar and God is still true. The revelation he gave you does not justify the way you're living. It justifies God but not you."

The second extraordinary argument that they were using in Paul's day and still sometimes do is: if my sin brings out God's grace and if my bad living brings out God's goodness, then why should he blame us? It is the old argument: surely it helps the world to understand God's grace if we sin, an argument we shall see coming up again in chapter 6. It is amazing that human beings can convince themselves of this, contending that because God's grace was manifest, that justifies our sin. We are going to have to learn that God can never justify sin. He can justify sinners, but never what they do. Let us get that absolutely clear. God will never approve or justify sin. He can't – he is righteous.

The Jews, of course, have the scriptures, so here Paul turns to them. They are proud of the fact that they have brought the Old Testament to the world. They revel in the fact that God chose them to reveal himself to everybody else, but the very scriptures which they have are full of observations that tell us how bad people are. We now have quotations from

Psalms 14, 53, 5, 140 (three quotes from that psalm) and 36, and in every case we have David observing human nature in the raw. This is what he says of them: "No one is righteous." Now that is King David, who was a man after God's own heart and a man in a position to think well of people, yet his observation of nature is that he has not met anyone in his life who is righteous. That is because he is measuring them by the righteousness of God. It is why Jesus objected to being called "good master". He said, "Why do you call me good? No one is good but only God." There is only one person who is good, who is righteous, and that is God. He will always be in the right. When he justifies a person, that person is now in the right. I love the Pidgin English Bible of New Guinea. They do not use the word "justified" or "justification". They have, "God 'e say 'im all right." That is justification" – "all right"; that is what the word "righteous" means – to be in the right in everything you do, everything you say, everything you think, everything you feel – to be in the right. Only God – the Father, the Son and the Holy Spirit – is always in the right.

So in the Psalms there are comments on "No one is righteous", and this is illustrated in two ways: first in their deeds, and, second, in their words. I was having my hair cut many years ago by a man called Chris. I can remember on one occasion he was cutting my hair and had got to a point behind my right ear and he suddenly said, "I am as good as anyone who goes to your church." I did not know what to say, and my little book on witnessing did not tell me how to answer. I was silent for a bit and he cut right around the back to behind my left ear. At that point he spoke again and said, "Well, perhaps not quite." By the time we had finished the haircut he was singing a different tune, but I said, "It doesn't matter. If you were as good as anyone who goes to our church that would make no difference. You are measuring yourself up by other people. That's fatal."

When we say, "He's a good man", or "she's a good woman," we are using a comparative term – compared to anyone else, but Jesus summed up human nature. "If you then, being evil, know how to give good gifts to your children, how much more will your heavenly Father give the Holy Spirit to those who go on asking him." It is a lovely promise. Here is another text: "Jesus would not put his trust in any man for he knew what was in man." Now if you have been brought up on a nice view of Jesus who trusted people and thought the best of them, you should study this scripture more carefully. Jesus would not trust anybody because he knew what was in people. That is quite a statement, and he said, "If you then, being evil, know how to give good gifts to your children, which of you, being asked for a bit of bread, would give them a stone or a scorpion?" You can read it all in Luke 11 – it is a very keen argument there.

Here is the point of utter difference between Christian and humanist thinking. To the humanist, people are basically good but know how to do bad things. To Jesus and to Christians, human nature is basically bad but knows how to do good things. There is a world of difference between those two diagnoses of our human condition. It is very important to ask yourself as a Christian whose view of human nature you accept. Do you accept that of the humanist, who says that people in their hearts are good? Have you read that amazing story of Anne Frank in the Netherlands, who was holed up in hiding by the Germans? I have a lovely letter from Anne Frank's father, because my daughter played the part of Anne in the play *The Diary of Anne Frank* and we got in touch with the father, who was still alive. At the end of that diary Anne wrote, "I believe that people are basically good." I thought, "I am afraid that's not true, Anne." She died in that faith – that after all the Germans did to her and her family, she believed that underneath basically human nature is good.

I underline that the Bible teaches that human nature is fallen. If you take the humanist line, that anybody is basically good but only does bad things, that is opposed to the Christ-like view of human nature, which is that we are evil but know how to do good things. There is the difference. The world wants the humanist view. Even some Christians want it, but, if you are going to have a realistic understanding, the fact is that the more you get to be like Christ, the nearer you get to him, the more you realise how bad you are and what your life might have been if God had not stepped in, and where you would have finished up. I don't know, but I know which direction it would have been. If God had not stepped into your life would you have gone up or down? That is the big question.

So the scriptures' commentary on human nature is that there is no-one righteous, no-one good enough for God's standards. Measure yourself by Jesus or by God, and you will realise the truth about yourself. Measure yourself by the people next door, or by people in the world who behead innocent people – measure yourself by them and you can come to the conclusion that, "Well, I'm a pretty good person." It is amazing how many people think that being kind to grandmother and the cat is being Christian. We know how to do good things, but we are basically bad people. That is why the wrath of God shows us up by taking the brakes off. We all owe gratitude for God's restraint on us through our parents, through the State we belong to, through our neighbourhood – which have all kept us back from doing worse things. When the brakes come off, then you see yourself as you really are.

Scripture not only talks about people's evil deeds, but their evil words. I think that finds me out and everybody else.

Would you like everything you have said about everybody else played on a voice recorder in the hearing of others? Somebody said, "If everybody knew what each had said of the other, there wouldn't be four friends left in the world." There were two women talking on a bus, and one said to the other, "I don't like her, and from all I've said about her I never will," which, when you think it through, is a priceless remark. We have all offended in word, and Jesus said that "for every idle word" we shall be brought into judgment.

An "idle word" is a word that was carelessly uttered, a word that slipped out, a word that revealed your real thoughts about something or someone. I could easily prove that I and just about everybody else have said the wrong thing at some time. James, in his letter, said, "This little tongue, it may be a small member, but it's set on fire by hell." More people have offended in tongue, not least in the things they have said in church set to music. I am afraid I have got to the stage where I will not sing a hymn if I don't mean it, because there are more lies sung in church than anywhere when you really look into what we sing – what we are saying to God set to music. It is really humbling. There was a dear man came to our church. He was the head of finance of a large airline and he came to church with his wife and three lovely boys. People would have said he was a good man, but I noticed that he never sang a hymn, though his family sang. I asked him about it: "Reg, why don't you sing a hymn?" He replied, "Because I don't mean it. I think it would be dishonest, and as a scout leader I promised to be honest. I'm not going to sing a hymn I don't mean." I really admired that man for that, because one day he started singing, and I knew that he meant it. He was a changed man, and he was the first man I ever baptised as a believer (along with my wife at the same time). I am not going to sing anything I don't mean. I commend that to you. It might spoil the singing in your church if you stop singing, but it would be more honest with God.

That little tongue is the most difficult thing to control in your body. A Church of England vicar said to his congregation, "I'm going to show you the part of my body that I have most difficulty in controlling." A deathly hush came over the whole congregation, then he made his point by sticking his tongue out. If you have sinned in no other way in your life, think about what you have said. The three classic questions to ask yourself before you speak are: Is it kind? Is it true? Is it necessary? Much of what we say won't pass those simple questions.

So it is not just our deeds but our words. So much damage has been done in words. "There is poison on our lips." Words are used by God. Most of the gifts of the Spirit are word gifts, but the devil also uses the tongue. Look at some of the most evil men who existed. Many of them had a gift of oratory and persuasion. Watch any film of Adolph Hitler. Speech was his biggest weapon, and he used it with power and great effect. It was poison. In fact, says Paul, "Our mouths are like an open grave," rotten and stinking. Then he mentions our feet. We sin with our feet. How do you do that? Well, your feet take you where you want to go. Now the Bible often says, "Beautiful are the feet of him who brings good tidings." Did you ever realise your feet are beautiful because they took you to someone who needed to hear your testimony? But the devil can use your feet too, to direct you into the wrong place.

The conclusion: no-one fears God. In that simple statement, David put his finger right on the root problem. It is true today that, even in church, the fear of God has often disappeared. The early Society of Friends were nicknamed "Quakers" because when they met for worship they trembled before God – they quaked. I have been in some worship sessions where I have seen people trembling before God.

"Fear God" is an idea that is so alien to some modern church people, but it is not just in the Old Testament. It is written right through the New. God says, "Don't fear those who can kill your body and do nothing worse. Fear him who can destroy body and soul in hell." He is not meaning the devil there. It means God. Who is afraid of God? You are only afraid of God if you have a real sense of sin, righteousness, and judgment. If there is one thing missing today it is the fear of God. We live in a day when his love has been so over-emphasised that fear has disappeared. I have written a book about that. As I have travelled around churches I have heard so much about the love of God and there is very little of fear of God, but he is a God to fear. As long as there is sin remaining in me I should fear God if I am not letting him deal with it, because there is a price to pay.

So the portion of scripture that begins, "No-one is righteous," ends with the conclusion, "No one fears God." Many of our politicians would be better in their job if they feared God. It is a fundamental emotion that is a healthy emotion. If it becomes a phobia it is unhealthy. We have many phobias and that is an exaggerated fear that paralyses. When my children were at a certain age, they came and said, "Daddy, can you get us some bicycles please?" I replied, "Not just yet." They said, "Well, everybody else in school has a bicycle." I tried to put them off a bit because we lived on a very dangerous road. I was passing on to them a phobia. What I should have done is passed on to them the real fear of traffic, a healthy fear, which made them careful, which anticipated trouble on the road. A phobia paralyses and means you can't go out on a bicycle at all.

Do you understand this? There is a healthy fear of God that makes us careful, that makes us aware of danger. There is a phobia of God which paralyses and you can't move. There are loads of phobias that people have: fear of open spaces, closed spaces, darkness, spiders, and so on. Those are irrational phobias. We are only born with two fears: the fear of falling and the fear of a loud noise. You can frighten a newborn baby with those two things; pretend to drop them or shout. Every other fear we have picked up either as children or even adults. Every other fear is picked up from others. Did you know that? The one fear that is so often missing is fear of God. If you fear cancer more than God, that has got your life out of order. People fear all kinds of things, but I very rarely meet anybody who is afraid of God. Yet, when you consider his power, his majesty, and above all his righteousness, they have plenty of reason to fear God.

I have to add there that there is one teaching that has taken away the fear of the Lord for many people, and it is summed up in four words: "once saved, always saved". I have noticed that has removed fear of God from people and given them a false security and a false complacency. We will have to face that later in chapter 11 of Romans where Paul clearly states that believers can lose their salvation. He could not have stated it more clearly. But I believe this issue has caused more Christians to stop fearing God than anything, so I wrote a book *Once Saved, Always Saved?* In it I mention eighty passages of Scripture in which we are warned not to lose our salvation. Many people have written to me after reading that book and have said, "Thank you, David, for restoring the fear of the Lord to me." It is a healthy fear, not a phobia, and that does not paralyse people, it makes them careful. We all need that fear of the Lord.

Finally, the last thing in this passage that Paul has to tell the Jews is: You have the scriptures and they say we have all sinned; you also have the statutes, the law. He adds two little asides to that statement. First, the law should be accusing you and help you to realise you are accountable to God. You should not be proud of the Ten Commandments unless you're keeping them all. There was a man in Scotland who said to his minister, "I am going out to visit the Holy Land for the first time. My ambition is to climb Mount Sinai and shout the Ten Commandments from the top." The minister said to this Scot, "You'd do far better to stay at home and keep them," which was a lovely way of telling him the law – don't be proud of having it; keep it.

It is to accuse you and bring you to the point where you cannot defend yourself. It is to silence people. It is when you study the law of God and what he requires that you are silenced. Silence in court is a healthy thing. It is also meant to bring conviction. That is why God gave the law – six hundred and thirteen laws in Moses, and he gave them all to prepare them for Christ because they would not be able to keep them and God knew that. He gave the law to arouse a sense of sin. That was its prime purpose. That is why it came before Christ and why that law was abolished in Christ. We shall see that also later in Romans.

John Wesley (whom I revere because of my ancestral connection with him and for his amazing ministry) was asked, "What is your method in evangelism? How come you lead so many people to Christ?"

Wesley replied, "When I go to a new town or village that I've never been before, I spend the first week or ten days preaching nothing but the law of God. When I begin to see some of them coming under conviction I begin to slip in a bit of the gospel until finally I'm preaching nothing but the gospel." That was a profound remark. So Wesley went round England preaching the law first to prepare people for the gospel. That is why we have been looking at this rather grim and even glum section of Romans. We have got to study that first. It is preparing the way for the beauty of the gospel.

So law was given first to the Jews, but to prepare them for the gospel. That is its purpose – and to face people with

God's high moral standards until they realise how far short they have fallen of the glory of God. That is the definition of sin here. Those who have fallen short of God's glory – now, no matter how good a jumper you are. Three men were stranded on a rock with the incoming tide. As the tide surged in, the shore seemed to go further and further. They realised that they would have to jump for it. One man jumped, and he managed to get halfway to the shore, then he sank in the water and drowned. The second man jumped, and he was within three feet of the shore, but he too drowned. The third man braced himself and really threw himself over, and he fell short by just a foot, and he drowned too. It does not matter how far you have jumped morally, if you have fallen short, that is the end. In other words, if you fall short of God's standards by a big lot or a little lot makes no difference. You are still a dead person.

We have realised at this point God's problem. People so search the Bible for an answer to their own problems that they miss the point that the real Bible is all about God's problem, which is very simple: rebellious kids. Praise God, he found a way of solving that problem, and in the next study we will get some better news.

3. JUSTIFICATION

ROMANS 3:21–5:21

A FOUNDATION OF FAITH (3:21-31)
   1. Gospel explained (21-26)
       a. Righteousness revealed
           i. Apart from but testified to by law (and prophets)
           ii. Through faith in Jesus Christ
       b. Grace given
           i. All have fallen short
           ii. Freely through Jesus' redemption
       c. Justification justified
           i. A sacrifice of atoning blood
           ii. A demonstration of justice
   2. Law excluded (27-31)
       a. Boasting banned
           i. Not law observed
           ii. But faith exercised
       b. Salvation standardised
           i. Only one God
           ii. Only one way to God (Jew and Gentile)
       c. Law legitimised
           i. Not nullified ii. But upheld

B FATHER OF FAITH (4:1-25)
   1. Faith credited (1-12)
       a. One man (Abraham)
           i. Not wages for works (obligations)
           ii. But gift for faith (offering)
       b. Any man (David)
           i. Sins not accounted
           ii. Circumcision not applicable
   2. Future promised (13-25)
       a. All men (nations)
           i. Not heirs through law (legacy of wrath)
           ii. But offspring through faith
       b. One man (Isaac)
           i. Reproduction (Sarah's womb)
           ii. Resurrection (Jesus' tomb)

C FRUIT OF FAITH (5:1-21)
   1. New future (1-11)
        a. Inspiring hope
               i. Of glory
               ii. From suffering
               iii. In love
        b. Increasing help
               i. Dying for his enemies
               ii. Living for his friends
   2. New nature (12-21)
        a. One man's disobedience (Adam)
               i. Made many sinners – condemnation
               ii. Sin reigned in death – before the law
        b. One man's obedience (Jesus)
               i. Made many righteous – justification
               ii. Grace reigned in life – after the law

PLEASE READ ROMANS 3:21–5:21

The first key word in this passage is "justification", a term that is straight from the law courts. It is used by the judge in a court when a man is found innocent and a case against him is dismissed. So it is equivalent to being declared innocent. Now how can it be that God could ever declare innocent those who have sinned in the way that we saw in the earlier chapters? It sounds an impossibility, but this is God's solution to the problem. It is to justify not what they have done but to justify them themselves and to say they are innocent. How can they be, when they are guilty?

Romans 3:21-31 sorts that out for us and tells us how God can remain just and be the justifier of sinners. How can he do it? God is so righteous that he must punish sin, or, to put it another way, God is too righteous to forgive anyone. It would be immoral for a just God to dismiss someone as innocent when he knows perfectly well they are not innocent – so how come? The answer is really very simple. God can only forgive sin when it has been paid for, when justice has been done. That can only happen when an innocent person is punished instead of the guilty. Then his justice has been satisfied, and the sinner has been justified, declared innocent.

We are at the heart of the gospel now. Quite simply, if there was one person who never should have been punished for sin it is the one sinless person, Jesus, who was punished. Now that, in the simplest way I can put it, has enabled God to change his attitude to sin from one of forbearance to one of forgiveness. The key words that begin the section are: but now. Whenever you find one of God's 'buts' in scripture it is terribly important. Something has happened which changes the whole situation. Until now, God has not forgiven sin – he could not offer forgiveness until now, he has taken a forbearing attitude. He has been overlooking sin. Quite literally, in one point in Acts 17, Paul tells the people in Athens that God has been winking at sin until now: but now. There is a huge difference between forbearing sin and forgiving it. God could not fully forgive sin until it had been paid for and paid for by an innocent person voluntarily accepting the punishment that was due to the guilty.

Now that is the most amazing thing! That is the heart of the gospel, and this section finishes by saying that God can be just and the justifier of the guilty. But there is a condition also. On God's part, justice has to be satisfied. The punishment of sin has to take place. The cross is not so much a demonstration of God's love as a demonstration of his justice. That is what it says here. You will never understand the cross until you grasp this – when you realise that the cross is a clear demonstration of his justice, that someone has to be punished to satisfy his justice, but in his *grace* (another new word that comes in this paragraph), sheer grace, his undeserved favour, he has sent his Son to bear the punishment on our behalf.

To put it as simply as I can: because Jesus took the punishment that was due to me, I can be forgiven my past. Justice has been satisfied. But that requires a condition on my part as well. It cannot happen automatically. It requires on my part *faith in Jesus*. "Faith" is another key word in this passage, occurring eight times in these few verses. On God's part. his justice has been satisfied by his Son, no less, who lived a perfect life, who did not deserve to die. On my part, I must put my faith in that person who died for me. Now this word "faith" – what does it mean? It does not mean just agreeing to what I have just been affirming. Faith *in* someone is much more than faith that someone. Real faith that saves the justified is not saying, "I believe that Christ was punished for my sin." That is believing *that*, it is not yet believing *in* him.

I was preaching in Hanover, Germany, on faith. I asked the congregation this question: "How many of you believe that I exist?" Everybody put their hands up. Then I continued, "That's a believing that someone exists or someone has done something for me. How many of you believe *in* me?" Only half a dozen people put their hands up. They had begun to see the difference between, on the one hand, believing that I am who I am and that I have done what I have done, and, on the other hand, believing *in* me, which is something different. There was a lot of hesitation now, but some half dozen people put their hands up, including a well-dressed lady in the front row. I can see her now. I said, "Now those of you who professed faith in me, I don't know if you have that faith or not. You have said you have faith in me, but you have given me nothing to prove that or to demonstrate that you really do believe in me." I said to this lady in the front row (she looked as if she would take a little teasing), "Now you raised your hand and you said you believe in me. I won't be able to know whether that is true until you do something to show me that you trust me. If you gave me your money to look after, I would know that you believed in me." A horrible hush came over the entire congregation. I was actually addressing the richest lady in Hanover. The whole church was horrified that I said, "Give me your money to look after, and I'll know you believe in me," but I meant it. I later found that she had paid for the lovely, brand-new church to be built in which I was speaking, but I had made the point.

Faith is showing someone by your act that you believe in them. You are doing that every day. If I get into a car that you are driving, I am believing in you. It is a matter of trust and obedience together. Faith combines both. If you believe in someone you will do what they tell you. If they say, "Get into my car," you will get into their car if you believe in them. Every time I get into a plane I am putting my trust in the pilot; I am believing that he will get me there. Getting on the plane is an act of faith. Now with faith in Jesus, you need to do something to show him that you trust him and that therefore you will obey him if he tells you to do something. That is faith in someone.

We are going to see in this study that Abraham is the classic example of someone who really put his trust in the Lord. He did not know Jesus at that time – Jesus had not been born – but he had faith in God. You know when he demonstrated that faith. That was when God not only gave him a son but told him to sacrifice that son. Now that was a terrific test of Abraham, and yet he went on with his preparation to sacrifice Isaac. A most significant statement was made afterwards. Now God did not let him sacrifice Isaac, but he tested him to the point of cutting his only hope of the future right off because only through Isaac would the promise be fulfilled. God said, "Now kill him for me." I can imagine them going up that hill when the young man said, "You've got the wood for the sacrifice, but you've got no animal to sacrifice. How are you going to offer a sacrifice to God?" I don't know if Abraham told him at that point, but sooner or later he must have realised that he was the sacrifice, and Abraham was willing to go right through with his death. It says (pay careful attention to this) after that, God said to Abraham, "Now I know that you fear me." In those words there is a most amazing revelation of God's ignorance of the future. God could know everything that Abraham could do, but he was not sure yet of what he would do in the circumstances. That really is a unique revelation of God's relationship to us. God does not know everything about your future in the sense that he does not know which decision you will make. He knows the consequences of those decisions, whether you say yes or no to him. He knows what can happen to you, but he does not know what will happen. Now that may come as a shock to you. The idea is so common that God knows everything that is going to happen and knows for sure which way you are going to decide before you decide, and yet here we have this phrase from God: "Now I know". Now God is sure of Abraham's faith. He was not sure before that, but when Abraham was willing to sacrifice Isaac, that was an assurance to God of Abraham's faith, which God was not sure of up to that point. Underline in your Bible those words "Now I know." They are so important. They tell you something about our God in relation to our freedom. We are free to choose. God has not predetermined our choice. Don't ever interpret predestination as predetermination. We will come back to that later in this letter.

That proved to God that Abraham trusted and obeyed him, and we shall see, later in chapter 4, why Abraham was willing to go through with that. There was a reason, and the reason lay in Abraham's faith. The reason for that faith lay in God's dealings earlier with him. To tell you the secret now before we get there, Abraham was willing to sacrifice Isaac because he already believed God could raise the dead. It was because of that faith in a resurrection from the dead that Abraham was willing to sacrifice Isaac. You are told this in Hebrews 11. If you wondered how on earth could Abraham bring himself to kill his own son as a sacrifice, the answer is that he had the faith to believe that God would raise him from the dead afterwards. That is an amazing faith for a man four thousand years ago. It was two thousand years before Jesus died and rose again that he had such a faith. He is the first man who believed that God could raise the dead.

Can you see how all this fits together? The one condition that God requires on our side to declare us innocent is faith in him – of the sort that Abraham had. Faith is a mixture of trust and obedience, or obeying because you trust. Therefore, when you trust someone you do what they tell you. When you go to the doctor and the doctor says, "Take these pills", you put your trust in the doctor – not when you are given the pill, but when you take them. You are saying, "I trust the doctor knows what I need, so I do what he tells me." If you go to the doctor and you don't do what he tells you, you really have no faith in him, no trust.

This word "faith" comes not only eight times in these few verses but sixteen times in the whole passage we are talking about. It is the key word in chapters 3–5. It is the key word in salvation, but it is not saying you *believe that*. It is *believing in the one who paid for your sins*, which means you *trust him and do what he tells you*. That is more than just saying the sinner's prayer. It is something much deeper. It is doing something that shows you trust the Lord and will do what he tells you. I hope that I have made that clear.

Romans 3:21–26 is a key passage in the whole letter, and goes to the very heart of the gospel. The heart of the gospel is the cross, the fact that your sins have now been paid for. Up to now, God forbore with sin. Forbearance means overlooking sin, accepting that you are a sinner but not declaring you innocent. But now sin has been paid for because (as he repeats here) all have sinned and come short, and therefore nobody can save themselves. That is like trying to lift yourself by pulling on your bootlaces. You cannot do it. You can never make yourself innocent. One of the tragedies of sin is that you lose your innocence, and you can never give it back to yourself again.

To illustrate that from the sexual sphere, as soon as you have had sexual intercourse with someone you are not married to, then you have lost your innocence, and you cannot give it back to yourself again. You know it in you. You have lost something. That is why God told us to save sex for marriage. You want to come to marriage innocent so that you can give the one you are marrying the best wedding present you could give, and that is your innocence. The beauty of that is that you will forever afterwards associate that pleasure with the one to whom you are married. That is God's plan, that we come to marriage both of us innocent, and therefore we will never mentally associate sexual pleasure with anyone else. That will hold you together for the rest of your life, because you experience that pleasure for the first time with the one to whom you are married for the rest of your life.

That is God's intention and you can see that young people are losing their innocence and will never be able to come to marriage without the memory of that first intercourse, which is tragic. They will then be subject to Satan's temptation of thinking of that other person while they are having sex with their spouse. You can understand God's rules of absolute chastity before marriage and absolute fidelity after marriage. They make for the happiest marriage. It is so sensible. When I talk to young people I beg them, "Don't lose your innocence. Keep it as a wedding gift for your partner, and forever afterwards that exquisite pleasure, and it is a pleasure, will be associated with that person and not with anyone else. That will keep you together for as long as you live. If you throw your innocence away, you will never know that." Tragically, you will have to ask God to cleanse your memory. The interesting thing is that God does cleanse your memory after your partner dies and you are then free, totally free in God's sight, to marry someone else, but that only happens when your partner dies. It does not happen if your partner is still alive and you marry someone else.

Faith in Jesus is a kind of final thing – that you give him

your trust and obedience from then on. On that condition, God declares you absolutely innocent. The first man who experienced that was Abraham. He was the first to whom God credited righteousness because of his faith. So the first thing is that *righteousness is something that God gives and we receive*. It is a righteousness from God, apart from the law, apart from good deeds, apart from earning. It is entirely free. It is through faith in Jesus Christ, in him as a person who has paid the penalty for you. By the way, this is the first mention of the Lord Jesus Christ in the letter. So far we have not mentioned him except right at the beginning when Paul said, "I'm a slave of Jesus." Now he is mentioned as the heart of the gospel. To say that Christianity is Christ is a cliché, but it is a fundamental statement. *To be a Christian is to have put your trust and therefore your obedience in this one person who paid the price of justice for you, which means that you have been bought with a price and that every act of forgiveness by God is written in the blood of Jesus*. It is forbearance up till then; forgiveness after then. So it is grace-given because all have fallen short of the glory of God, as we have seen. Whether you have fallen short by thirty percent, sixty percent, ninety percent or even ninety-nine percent, you have fallen short and therefore you need the free gift of grace. That is what you receive when you believe in Jesus.

Paul writes about Jesus' redemption. The word "redeem" always means to pay for someone's freedom, to ransom them. If you redeem something that you took to the pawnbroker, you have got to pay to get it back again. That is called redeeming what you gave to the pawnbroker and raised some money on. You give something to a pawnbroker. He gives you money for it. You can spend that money or pay debts with it, but you will not redeem your property. It is yours but it does not belong to you. You can't use it. It is still yours; it is in your name, but you will redeem it when you pay the price to get it back. That is what has happened. That is why we talk about the redemption. It means more than rescuing. It means paying the price to rescue. Jesus redeems us by paying the price with his own life, with his own blood. Forgiveness is not cheap. It always costs someone heavily. It cost Jesus everything, but the redemption is offered to us as a free gift. He paid; it is free for us. That is grace.

Thirdly and lastly in this section, God is now able to be just and justifier of sinners. He is just because he made someone pay. He gave his own Son to do the paying, so never think that Jesus was rescuing us from a God reluctant to forgive. It was God who thought it up, and it was God who sent his Son, and at one stage must have said, "Son, are you willing to go and pay for the sins of the whole world?" That raises one question: that, for the slightest sin, death is the penalty, which always seems a bit fierce, a bit over the top, that God should for just one little lie pronounce death as the sentence. There is a reason for that. Here I am going back to the end of chapter 1 where it says that death is the penalty for the slightest sin. The reason is really very simple. If God did not pronounce death as the penalty for even the slightest sin it would mean that he was making evil eternal; that he was colluding with us in spoiling his universe forever. Death must be the sentence to sin to stop it becoming eternal. Do you follow me in that? That is why for the slightest sin that I have committed God has to impose the death sentence. In other words, he has to say that he will now set a limit to the life of that sin. That is the perfection of God, his righteousness, that he will not allow sin to go on forever. Therefore he has imposed the death sentence and Jesus has taken the death sentence. It had to be that death, that horrible death, that lonely death, that painful death, because that was the penalty for any sin. It all makes sense once you look at it this way and it all fits together.

Alas, one of the leading evangelical broadcasters in England has said the most blasphemous thing about Jesus' death. He calls himself an evangelical and he is often on the television or radio – and he said publicly in England, "If God punished Jesus for our sins that is a classic case of child abuse." That statement has gone around evangelicals in England from this teacher and leader. His Son gladly accepted that, as Isaac had accepted his father's will to kill him. Funnily enough, it was on the top of the same mountain that Abraham offered Isaac or nearly killed him and saw a ram, a male lamb, with its head caught in the thorns. God said, "You can substitute for your son Isaac that lamb." All this was prefiguring in an amazing way the Lamb of God with his head caught in the thorns, a crown of thorns, on that same mountain, who was the substitute sacrifice for all of us. Can you see that link? What an amazing picture! That is one of the things God was constantly doing, showing us in the Old Testament how he was going to operate in the New.

This excludes the law. In 3:27–31, all law is excluded. Keeping the law is excluded. It is either grace that forgives and declares innocent, or it is trying to keep the law. You cannot mix them up. Boasting is therefore banned – because it is not the law observed which brings pride to you, but the law by-passed, and faith exercised. There is no pride in believing in someone else. That is no virtue, and yet it has been reckoned in your account as righteousness. Now this means that salvation has been standardised. If there is only one God, there can be only one way to that God. The word "one" is important here. If there is one God, there must be only one way to that God. Therefore there is no way to God by the law now. There is only one way, and that is the way of faith in his Son, Jesus.

Yet Paul says, "Does this nullify the law?" "No," he says, "The law is upheld." Then he just does not explain that at this point. He will explain it later in Romans, and we shall get the explanation. But in some amazing way the law is cancelled as a way to God, it has not been nullified, because this is God's way to having his law kept. We shall find later in the epistle that love is the fulfilling of the law and that if you love your neighbour you don't steal from them, you don't murder them and you don't bear false witness against them. There is another way of fulfilling the law now, and the way of faith in Jesus is going to get the law done without you realising it. It is quite an amazing thing. God did not cancel the law. He has found a better way of helping people to keep it – wanting to keep it. He is going to write the law, not on tablets of stone but in their hearts where they will be motivated to do what the law required. That is all in the future. Paul will say later that the law is good, holy, righteous. It is not a bad thing, the law of God, but when you use it as a way to God, it becomes a barrier.

Now we turn to chapter 4. Abraham is the father of faith. Bear in mind he is writing to the Gentile believers of Rome. The word "faith" comes fifteen times in this chapter. The word "credited" comes in ten times, so we have found the key words. Faith is credited in God's accounts (instead of righteousness) as righteousness. That means that to get into God's good books all you need is faith. If you are trusting in his Son who paid the debt for you, then you are credited as a righteous man or woman. It is an accounting term, a term for adding up accounts, and there is a credit and a debit side. The debit side is now vanished because the debt has been paid, justice has been satisfied, but on the credit side is your faith. That is all God requires to declare you innocent. Case dismissed; your judgment has taken place and you are free, an innocent person. That is again the heart of the gospel. Faith has been credited in the account in heaven of your life. It is on the positive good side, and it is all you need to be declared innocent by God. What a gospel we have! What good news that is to people who are up to their eyes in debt – to be told the debt is cancelled!

The way they cancelled debts in the Bible days was to take the bill, the invoice, and to fold it over and nail it to the wall. So if you owed money to a grocer or a carpenter, your debt to him would be pinned up on the wall of his shop, and when that debt is cancelled he would fold the paper over and drive the nail through both sides of the paper. It is cancelled, it has gone, and that is exactly what Paul says in another letter where he writes that Jesus took your debt and he nailed it to the cross and the debt is gone. If you really realise that, the relief that comes when the debts are paid for is sheer joy. Someone will explode with joy if you cancel their debt for them, and once again at the cross your debt has been cancelled, folded over and nailed to the cross, says Paul.

Well now, this idea of faith credited, Abraham discovered that. He was the first to do so – that therefore he was not being said to be righteous because of good deeds that he had done. If it had been that way, he would get wages for it. God would have been under obligation to pay him. He would have got God in his debt. You would be amazed how many ordinary people think they can get God in their debt and that they have done enough good deeds to get him in their debt and that he is obligated to take them to heaven, that he is obliged to, under contract to – what a dreadful thought! It is not wages for works, or Abraham could have boasted. It was not an obligation. It was a free-will offering to Abraham. He did not have to earn it in any way or deserve it. It was freely offered. It was not wages for work, but a gift for faith.

King David took up the same thought in the Psalms. This blessing of having your debts paid off is for anyone. In the Psalm, he said, "Blessed is the man whose sins are not counted against him." That is the debit side of the heavenly account, and it is a lovely thought. Because of this, because Abraham discovered this before he was circumcised and before he circumcised anyone else, it means that circumcision has nothing to do with being credited as righteous in God's sight. That is one in the eye for Jews, or one in the ear for them in this letter. With the faith that was credited to Abraham, along with it went a future that was promised to him. The rest of the chapter 5 is about that promise. *Abraham believed the promises of God.* That again is part of trusting someone and therefore obeying them – that you are relying on something they have promised to you. You are taking them at their word, and you are trusting them to keep it.

All business is built on trust, and once trust goes, business becomes impossible. In every business transaction you are putting trust in someone else. You are trusting that what they have promised to do for you or what they have promised to give you, they will keep. Alas, in human business there are many disappointments. Businesses go bankrupt and their debts are not paid, but normal business would be impossible without trust in the other person's word. Sadly, while it used to be the case that a man's word was his bond and you could trust him, that is no longer a proverb in the financial centre of London. You cannot trust everybody today. It has done a lot of harm to British business that a man's word is not his bond any more and can be proved to be untrustworthy. Business in London is more on a knife edge now, but it used to be solidly based on a simple fact. If a man gave his word to you, you could trust that. That built up the riches of London.

But, you see, it is the same with God. You take God at his word, and you trust him to keep a promise. That is what Abraham did and he proved it again and again. Because of that he was promised a future. When Abraham trusted God's word he saw miracles happen. God made promises to

Abraham which Abraham never saw fulfilled. He died before they were fulfilled. He was promised the same amount of children as there are stars in the sky. That is six thousand – in Abraham's day the naked human eye could only see six thousand. We now know there are millions up there, but he did also promise him that his children would be as the sand of the sea. Abraham did know that the sand on the seashore is billions. He was promised billions of children. Today that promise is being fulfilled. There are a billion and a half professing Christians in our world, and because they share Abraham's faith or at least they profess to, they are his children.

Abraham died. Do you know how many sons he had when he died? He had nine. It is there in Genesis. You knew he had Isaac; you knew he had Ishmael first, an illegitimate son by his wife's maidservant. That was never God's will, but he couldn't wait patiently for God's promise. When God made a promise to Abraham, Abraham was way past the age for having children. So was Sarah, and she had been barren all her life. They were in their nineties and God promised Abraham, "You will have a son." Abraham believed it and then his faith faltered, and his wife's suggestion was, "You'd better have sex with my maid and that's the only way you'll get a son." Look at the result of that! In the descendants of Ishmael and the descendants of Isaac today there is no love lost. That one act of Abraham has caused untold tension in our modern world because Ishmael has had many sons and so has Isaac. The hatred (almost) between the Arab Muslims and the Jews in Israel is all due to that. It goes right back to Abraham's attempt to speed God up, and listening to his wife's logic. But he regretted it and he got back to faith. He and his wife got older and older and then Isaac was born. That was proof to Abraham that God could raise the dead because, as we are told in chapter 5 here, Sarah's womb was as good as dead, and Abraham's sexuality was as good as dead at that age. Yet God brought life from two sexually dead people. It was that which gave Abraham belief in the resurrection of the dead. For us, we have a fundamental faith in the God who brings life from death. For us it is not Sarah's womb that proves that, but Jesus' tomb proves it. It is the same faith. It is the same total trust in a God who can raise the dead. It was that faith that led Abraham to sacrifice Isaac, or to be willing to in later life, that proved to God that Abraham really did fear God. "Now I know" – remember that. So that God promised Abraham a future not only to have a son, but to have so many children that nobody could count them like the sand on the seashore, like the stars in the sky. Now that has been fulfilled. We can see it in our day, and therefore we have faith in the God who can bring life from the dead.

He did it with his Son, Jesus, after he paid the penalty. It was God who raised Jesus. Jesus didn't raise himself. God raised him. It was an act of creation. God actually wiped out the old body of Jesus in the tomb and gave him a brand-new body outside the tomb. We don't always realise that resurrection is not resuscitation. God did not restore the old body of Jesus in the tomb. He did not bring the old body to life, or that body would have died again later of old age. The body that Jesus came out of the tomb with was not the body he went into the tomb with. That body completely disappeared, leaving the grave clothes wound up. That was the beginning of our faith that God can make a new creation and that the old creation will pass away. That is a gigantic thing to believe – that this world will disappear one day and God will make a new planet Earth and a new space. That is amazing! We are the only people in the world who believe that – that the God who created this old universe is going to make it vanish and in its place build a brand-new one.

Do you believe that? It is at the end of your Bible and it is a promise of the future.

Abraham again is the classic case of a man who believed that what God promises to do, he will do. Even if you never see it in your lifetime, he will do it. One of the verses that always moves me is in the middle of Hebrews 11 where, after describing the faith that the people of God had in the Old Testament, it says, "These all died still believing." Most of them never saw what God had promised them, but they died trusting in it. We are told that they will come back to life in the resurrection with us and then we will see all those promises fulfilled. That is faith. It is believing that God will do what he said he will do even if you do not live to see it. You die like Abraham, still believing in what God promised. God had promised him descendants, a land, and a city that he could live in forever. Because of that new city which God had promised, he was content to live in a tent after he retired. As a businessman in Ur of the Chaldees, he had lived in a two-storey brick house with modern fireplaces. They have discovered those houses, and they are amazing. They were modern, centrally heated, with brick walls. Those were the houses that Abraham lived in. I showed my wife a photograph of one that has been unearthed in Ur of the Chaldees. It was a room with one of the fireplaces and when she looked at it I asked her, "What do you think of that house? Would you like to live there?" She commented, "It's a bit old-fashioned, isn't it?" I said, "Yes, it's four thousand years old." Abraham left a comfortable brick house when he was an old man and he was willing to live in a tent because God had promised him a city one day. He died still in that tent. He never lived to see it, but he died believing that God would do it.

So here we have a future promise of the whole world. God promised Abraham: the whole world will be yours, not just part of the promised land in it. That is a whole world – nations. Kings would be born from Abraham. Huge promises! Only God could have kept them. Abraham died without seeing them, but he was still believing when he died. God will do it. Statistically, I am near death and I may die before seeing God's promises fulfilled, but I know he will fulfil them. I believe in a new heaven and a new earth and a new body for me to live in it. I may die before I see all those things, but I know they will happen. I know I will be there, because I believe I will have a new resurrected body. Jesus promised it. That is good enough for me! It should be good enough for every Christian. What promises we have received!

Abraham was outstanding in his faith. He believed everything God told him he would do and he stuck by it. He died believing, not seeing, but he died believing that he would inherit the whole world. That's amazing! I so look forward to meeting Abraham, don't you? A man of faith, and that's the most important thing about Abraham that you'll ever read. He believed and his faith was credited to him for righteousness. He was the first man to hear the verdict, he's innocent; he's justified. The first person God ever said that about was Abraham. If we share his faith, then we share his inheritance. We become sons of Abraham and therefore his heirs.

That word is now going to come into this letter. We are not only sons of God by faith, we are heirs of the world. "Blessed are the meek, for they shall inherit the earth." You may die without inheriting anything, but you can die believing that you are going to inherit the earth. That is your legacy that God has left you. One day he will keep that promise. He does not promise to do it in your lifetime, but he has promised to do it, and therefore faith grasps what is not seen and makes it real. It is the evidence of things hoped for and, for the Christian, "hope" is not a wishy-washy word but a very strong word. It means I am certain of the future, I am absolutely sure that God will do what he has promised. He is going to bring his Son back to earth. He has promised to do that and I am absolutely sure of that. He has promised to create a new heaven and a new earth, and he has promised that I can live in it. He will keep that promise even though I die still believing. So the future was promised to the father of faith. Faith was credited and therefore the future was promised. They will not be heirs of Abraham through law, but through grace. It will be an offering through faith, which will be inherited. As I have mentioned, Abraham believed in reproduction. We believe in resurrection, but they are the same thing – God bringing life from the dead. It happened in his own sexual life, and it will happen in our own physical life too.

So we move on to the fruit of faith, its results. What will all this mean in practice? Will it make any difference to life now, or will we just have to wait for all the promises of God to be fulfilled. The good news is that we have both a new future and a new nature. We can experience those already. Look at the key words in 5:1–21. There is the fruit of faith. Look what we have got. We already have *peace* with God now. We don't need to wait for that. Shalom is a lovely word (*salaam* in Arabic). It means harmony with yourself, harmony with other people, harmony with nature and, above all, harmony with God. You can have it now – it is the present result of faith.

Not only do we have peace with God, we have *access* to God. We have got that now, long before we inherit the earth. Particularly in Arabic countries, a king is someone you can approach. If you are a citizen of the kingdom, you have a right to come into the king's private throne chamber and present your petition. You must have seen pictures of Arabs, particularly, queuing up in a king's room with petitions, which they can present to him. They have access. It is one of the unusual features of Arabic culture that every citizen has access to the king. As Christians we have access to the King of kings. You can go to him at any time and in any place with a petition and ask him for help. That is a privilege in the now, not something you have to wait for or may still be believing will happen when you die. Access to the throne of grace is something you can enjoy every day.

A little girl was going home from Sunday school, singing a chorus she thought she had learned, and she ran down the street singing, "God is still on the phone; God is still on the phone." She had got it right. You don't need a mobile phone to get through to God. You can get through to God now in an instant. Wherever you are, whatever is happening, you have access to the throne of grace. What a sheer privilege! Non-Christians don't have that access. They may say prayers, but they don't have access. The Holy of Holies is now wide open. The curtain that shut off the Holy of Holies from the ordinary people, even from the ordinary priests, has been ripped in two, from top to bottom, when Jesus died. We now have total access into the Holy of Holies of heaven, for the earthly tabernacle and the earthly temple were only copies of what is really happening up there in heaven. We have access! I just can't get over this. What a privilege! Why don't we use it more?

One of the things we already have is hope. It is interesting that Romans begins with an emphasis on faith, and now we move into an emphasis on hope. Later we shall move into an emphasis on love. "Now abideth faith, hope and love." I would conclude: now abides faith, hope and love, but of these the most neglected is hope. We live in a world where people are without God and therefore without hope. They are not without wishful thinking, but (in English anyway) "hope" is a very uncertain word. We hope it will be fine tomorrow. (Well, if you live in England we are always talking about the weather, and we are always disappointed with it. We hope it's going to be fine and then it rains. It is so unpredictable.) We hope to avoid cancer. We hope for a better job. We hope, but these earthly hopes are not sure at all.

The word "hope" in the Bible, the Greek word *elpis*, means to be absolutely certain. We have been given a hope to live by now. We have this certainty of the future to live by. It is not wishful thinking. It is not hoping we will have a good holiday. It is not even hoping for heaven in the sense that maybe we might get there after we die. "Christian hope is an anchor to the soul," says the letter to the Hebrews, and an anchor is something that goes down to the bottom of the sea, hooks on to something and holds the ship steady. Christian hope is an anchor to hold you steady when you are going through bad times, when you are going through storms, when the wind is battering you and threatening to blow you onto the rocks. In circumstances like that, you have an anchor that holds firm, a hope for the future that will not be destroyed by anything that happens to you.

Having talked to saints either under persecution or suffering terribly from fatal disease, I know – I have seen those who have a certain hope of the future can see it through. They have got an anchor deep down that holds the ship in the same place whatever forces are battering above. Hope is a wonderful thing to live by, and you can live by it when it is sure and certain. You may not see it yet, but when you know it is coming that makes a whole difference to how you live. When you are sure that Jesus is coming back, that makes a difference to how you live life today and will have a profound effect on what you can face. Paul actually goes on to say that you can rejoice in suffering, knowing that suffering will only produce more hope. It has a way of working like this: that suffering will produce patience, and patience will produce character, and character will produce hope so that you can rejoice in bad times. When you are really going through it and feel under it, your hope will be made stronger by it. I have seen that happen, but only in Christians who are sure of the future. Their hope comes out brighter and stronger and better after they have really been through it.

We have peace with God, we have access to him and we have hope that we can live by that will anchor us to the rock below. What else have we got? We have got love shed abroad in our hearts. Here is the amazing thing (and for the first time the Holy Spirit is mentioned), it is through the Holy Spirit that God's love is shed abroad in your heart. You find yourself with love for the most surprising people, people you never loved before, people you don't like. What benefits there are from faith! It has all come out of faith in Jesus. We are listing the benefits. Not only is there inspiring hope, but also a hope of glory. That is the third part of salvation. Justification is the first part, sanctification is the second, and glorification is the third. The hope of glory – we are going to shine with glory such as Jesus had when he was transfigured on the mountain in front of Peter, James and John. That is glory. It is shining; it is splendour.

A pop singer, Gary Glitter, has been in trouble in old age. What a name for a pop star! He wore sequined costumes – he shone with sequins. Once I was preaching on Daniel, where Daniel says, "The righteous will shine like stars," and I said, "Gary Glitter won't get a look-in. When you are glorified, you will shine like a star, and it won't ever get old and fade." A recording of that sermon went to the UN Headquarters in Paris near the Eiffel Tower. In that place there was a New Zealander who had been a member of our church, but in Paris he started a Bible study group in the UN building there. He got about a dozen people along. He played a recording of one of my sermons each week to this little group. That was not the only group to do that, but he played that recording of Daniel where I said, "Gary Glitter will fade, but you will shine like stars." I was trying to be clever, trying to be appropriate, or trying to be relevant. Sitting in the little circle of a dozen people in Paris was Gary Glitter's mistress. She was not listening to my recording. She was not interested until she heard "Gary Glitter", then she got interested, and her ears pricked up. By the end of that talk, she belonged to Christ. You never know, a little stray word can be used by God in the most unexpected way.

Does it thrill you, the hope of glory? It is a hope in suffering because that will produce more hope for you, and it is a hope in love that has been shed abroad in your heart. Who says there are no benefits now to a life of faith? All this is yours in this world and in this life. There will be increasing help for you from Jesus himself. Here comes an argument about future salvation. Paul says, "If we have been justified by his blood, how much more will we be saved...." Notice the "will" – future salvation, "How much more will we be saved by his life?" The tragedy of focusing on the death of Christ all the time is that you miss out on the "How much more will we be saved by his life?" The resurrection means more to us than his death. His death was wonderful. It enabled us to be justified and declared innocent, but how much more will we be saved by the risen, ascended Christ – now at the right hand of the Father, taking our prayers and presenting them to the Father on our behalf.

I wrote a short book entitled *Where is Jesus Now, and what is He Doing?* It is really saying: don't believe that Jesus is still on earth and somewhere in your heart a little Jesus. He is up there, he is at the right hand of the Father. The Holy Spirit has taken his place on earth. That is why you don't receive Jesus now. You receive the Holy Spirit who is his deputy on earth, but we have Jesus now on high at the right hand of the Father presenting our cause. He is our advocate. If a Christian sins, we have an accuser in heaven. Satan says, "There you go. There's one of your children sinning, God. Calls himself a Christian, calls himself a godly man, and look at him." Whenever we sin, there is an accuser in heaven and that is where the devil is. He has access to the heavenly places until he is thrown down to earth at a stage in future history. We have an accuser listing our sins at the same time we have an advocate up there to plead our cause. That is one of the things Jesus is doing for you right now. He is interceding for you now; praying for you when nobody else is praying for you—now. I am just amazed at chapter 5. I have got all this now and what there is yet to come! The mind just boggles.

So we have increasing help from him who died, not for his friends, not for good people, but for his enemies. "Greater love has no man than this," said Jesus, "that a man lay down his life for his friends." That is quoted so often on monuments, remembering the dead in two world wars. Did you ever hear of a British man who died for the Germans during World War II? I never did. I heard of many who died for their colleagues and their country and for a good cause, but I have only ever heard of one person who died for his enemies, and that is Jesus. What love he must have had to die for those who rebelled, who hated him! That love is shed abroad in your heart. So it was his death for his enemies and now his life for his friends. Don't forget that last bit. It is not just his death that saves you, it is his life! How much more will you be saved by his life? It does not refer to his life before he died, but his life after he rose, his present life. How much more will you be saved – now and in the future – by his life?

Do you know why he is coming again? According to

Hebrews 9 he is coming to bring salvation to those who are waiting for him. I am looking forward to being saved. Salvation is future. Out of past, present and future tenses of the verb saved – you have been saved, you are being saved, you will be saved – the emphasis of the New Testament is on the future. There is more about your future salvation than your past. I react negatively when someone uses in conversation the past tense of saved. They tell me, "We had ten people saved last Sunday," or, "I was saved twenty years ago at a Billy Graham Crusade." Every evangelical I talk to only uses the word "saved" in the past tense, as if it is all over and all finished. It is not. It has only just begun.

I had that reaction when teaching in Singapore. Somebody used the word "saved" to me and I said, "You mean they began to be saved." They looked a bit surprised when I said that. I began to be saved when I was seventeen, but it was only the beginning of my salvation. I will be saved. I look forward to being saved. When Jesus comes back, that will be when I will be saved, fully saved, completely saved. My body is not saved yet. It still bears the marks of my past life, but the redemption of my body is coming when Jesus gets back. My body will be saved. This one is going to rot in a tomb.

I am not going to be cremated. I want to be buried, and I have chosen the spot because when you bury someone it looks as if you are planting them in the earth, and what you plant in the earth will spring forth. I am not against cremation, but Christians have always preferred burial (like the Lord) and look forward to coming out of the grave. Now don't get me wrong, God can raise up a new body from ashes as well as dust. He is the Creator and he will do it, so it does not say that if you get cremated he is not going to raise you. Don't believe that, and don't you dare say, "David Pawson said that." I prefer burial. It is interesting that cremation has had more serious psychological effects in terms of ongoing grief than burial ever does because it seems somehow, to some people (and it may be neurotic) they believe they have destroyed their loved one, whereas if you plant them in the earth you have not destroyed the body, you have planted it.

Now we come to a most extraordinary section, vv. 12–21. Here is a very simple truth which many find difficult to accept. The truth is that, through one man's single act of disobedience, death has come to the entire human race, and through one man's act of obedience has come justification for the human race. The one man whose disobedience we remember is Adam. If you find it difficult to accept that one man, Adam, brought death to everybody else, you will find it just as difficult to believe that one man's obedience has brought life to a new human race. The two go together. We have become so individualistic in our thinking that we think that each person is an island living to himself – so how can I be blamed for what Adam did? There is a pride in us that wants to be responsible for ourselves and say, "I did it my way." That is the national anthem of sinners. We are meant to do it in Jesus' way.

We are corporate beings. You were inside Adam when he did what he did. You were literally in his body. You are descended from him. You get your DNA from him and therefore his one act of disobedience brought death to reign over the entire human race. Human nature says, "That's not fair", but then you might also say of Christ dying for your sins: "That's not fair, Lord." There is such a thing as corporate humanity, and in one man, Adam, we fell. The result was sin and death. This means, quite simply, that death is not natural to human beings. Science cannot prove why we have to die. At some point our bodies stop replacing cells that are dying with new cells, and we begin to wind down. Scientists can tell you how it happens, but they cannot tell you why. I challenge a scientist to tell me:

why is there that process whereby the capacity of our body to renew itself begins to fade, your teeth get fewer and your hair gets thinner. Your body is winding down. It has been said that every heartbeat is a drumbeat on the road to the grave.

Man is born to die as the sparks fly upward. A writing of the Jews between the Old and New Testaments says this, "Oh Adam, what have you done? For though it was you who sinned, the fall was not yours alone, but ours also who are your descendants. Oh Adam, what have you done?"

Then we come to the final statement and the most difficult of all to understand. From Adam's one act, death spread to all men because all men sinned. Now I want you to get the meaning of that phrase. You must get this phrase right in your understanding to understand the rest. Some have thought it means, "Because all men repeated Adam's folly and did the same kind of thing" or, rather, "...followed Adam's example". That is not what it means. It is true that we have all followed his example and touched things we were told not to touch. You tell a child not to touch a thing and see what happens. It is true, there is an old Adam in your child – but that is not what it means. Secondly, there are those who have thought that it meant that we all inherit Adam's nature, and that therefore because we have his nature, we all sin – but it does not even mean that, though that is true. One of the difficulties of having children, the tragedy, is that you pass on to them a sinful nature. You can't help but do so. "In sin did my mother conceive me" doesn't mean the sex act was sin, it means that she could only pass on to me a sinful nature. That is true too, but it is not what this phrase means.

What it does mean is this, and I am afraid your mind will find this difficult to accept at first. The natural mind, the unbelieving mind, cannot possibly accept it: that in Adam in fact we all did sin; that *in that one act, the whole of humanity was included* – that if no other sins had ever been committed, the whole human race had in fact sinned in one man. That is a concept you find difficult to believe, yet Paul is going to build on that understanding. Can I explore it a bit? It is obviously true that all of us were physically in Adam at that time because from his seed the human race sprang, so that literally we were all in his body. Everyone in your church was in Adam's body at that time, and the only reason we are here and have life today is because his seed was passed down to us through human reproduction. You have within your body the seed of Adam, and he had you in his body. But it is not only true physically, it is true spiritually.

The whole human race was in Adam at that point, and therefore when he committed that one sin, the whole human race sinned. We all sinned—that is why death spread to everybody. That is why death can affect a baby who has never sinned because that baby is part of the human race that has sinned in Adam. Long before a baby knows temptation, long before a baby has reached the age of responsibility, that baby can die, and the reason why it can is just this: that baby sinned in Adam. The whole human race sinned in Adam. Death is a sentence that is passed upon the whole human race because of one man's act.

Can we go further and illustrate this in the way that Paul does? He says you know that sin, being a transgression of the law, depends on the law that you are given. Adam was given a law, "Thou shalt not touch that tree of knowledge of good and evil." That was his law. Now he broke it; death came to him. Now from that point, of course, people being turned out of the garden of Eden had no opportunity to break the law given to Adam. The law given to Adam could not be broken again; it had been broken once, and the Ten Commandments and the rest of the law of Moses were not given until many years later. So there was a gap between the law given to Adam and the law given to Moses, and technically in that period there was no law of God to break. Therefore, technically, sins could not be counted as transgressions in the law over that period, and yet people who had no law died, and they died because the sentence was on the race – it was on mankind. All men sinned in Adam.

Now you can argue against that. You can say, "It's not fair." You can say this, that, and the other. You can say, "I just can't accept that," but facts are against you. The fact is that the most innocent people face death; that even an innocent baby can die, and God never intended that, and it is because of Adam that that happens. So the facts are there, and the facts are that there is not a man or a woman or a child who doesn't face death. It was all because of one man, and his act of disobedience once, and in Adam all sinned. Therefore, death spread to all people. Now you may say, "Surely, that is misinterpreting the phrase 'because all sinned'. Why can't it just mean 'because everybody copied him'?" Well I will show you in a moment, because now we turn to the other side of this: on exactly the same principle, because of the make up of our human race, because we are all one, because we are bound together, because we were all in Adam, because of that: *through one man's act of obedience, at one time, everybody related to him as righteous can have life.*

Now you cannot have it both ways. If you say, "It's not fair or right for everybody to have death because of one man's act of disobedience," then I say to you, "You will never be able to share in the life that everybody has because of one man's act of obedience." It goes together. You can have both or neither in your thinking, but if you can see that this is in fact how the human race does work, and that because of one man's disobedience the whole human race dies, we can now see that because of one man's act of obedience it is also possible for all who are related to *him* to have life.

Now go back to that phrase "because all sinned". If you

take that to mean, "Because all people sinned, all copied Adam's sin and therefore deserve to die," then you must interpret the rest to mean that we can have life by copying Christ's righteousness – and then the whole thing becomes ridiculous because you never can. The whole point of the argument is that one man's sin was enough to bring death to you all, therefore one man's righteousness is enough to bring life to you all. Do you see how it hangs together? You cannot believe the second unless you believe the first. Unless you believe that we all have death because of one man's single act of disobedience, we cannot believe that many can have life because of one man's single act of obedience. Yet that is the truth. I have life, not because I have copied Christ's righteousness, but *because I am in Christ*. Just as my body dies, not because I have copied Adam's sin, but because I was in Adam. You see the difference?

Therefore, all of us are either in Adam or in Christ. We are either going to die because of Adam or we are going to live forever because of Christ, and it will not be because we *copied* them, but because we were *in* them. Now here is a very deep and important truth that is going to lead straight into chapter six: *If you are in Christ, then do you realise that on the hill called Calvary, you died, you were crucified?* That is what you are going to have to realise if you are going to understand Romans 6. If I read Genesis 3 and the account of the garden of Eden and how Adam disobeyed and took that fruit, I must read that story and say: "On that day I took that fruit. On that day I was in Adam because I am descended from him and related to him and therefore I did that."

When I read the story of Christ being put to death I say: "On that day they drove the nails in, they were driving the nails into me. I died. I have been crucified with Christ, and I have been raised with Christ three days later." Now do you see how the truth is going to follow through in Romans chapter 6? In Adam – death; in Christ – life; in Adam I shared his sin and therefore death spread to me, and in Christ I shared his death and resurrection, and therefore life comes to me. It is not because I copy Adam or copy Christ, it is because I am *in* Adam or Christ that these things happen.

Therefore there is a comparison. "Adam," says Paul, "was a type of him who was to come. Adam was a pattern of Christ." Here was Adam at the beginning of the human race, and because the whole human race was in Adam, the entire race that spread from him was subject to death.

Then somebody else came into that race: Christ. He actually died; he went through the death of the human race, but he rose from the dead. Therefore from Christ there is a new humanity that will have life for evermore. Now then, where are you? If you are just in Adam then the certain thing I can say about you is that you are going to die. But if you are in Christ then you are having eternal life, and even the physical death you still have to go through because your body is still in Adam cannot touch your life. God will raise you up to eternal life. In Adam, in Christ, and from both, there come two humanities: a humanity under death and a humanity under life.

Look at the contrast this brings. For the rest of the chapter Paul draws contrast after contrast between what happens to you because of Adam's sin and disobedience and what happens to you because of Christ's obedience and righteousness. Adam's sin robbed you of life; Christ's righteousness gives you life. Adam's one act led to the condemnation of all; Christ's one act leads to justification – acquittal. Adam's one act led to slavery because death reigned over the human race. Do you realise how that death is your "king" in Adam – a tyrannical king? Every one of us is on our way to our own funeral. In Christ you are free.

Where does the law come in all this? When God gave

the Ten Commandments, what did that do? Frankly, it came to those who were under death, and it made the situation worse because when the law came, sin increased – people knew what laws to break. However, the tide of sin rose but the lifeboat of salvation went up with it. Sin increased but grace abounded, so that God was always on top of the situation. Finally, just at the right time – when it had got to its worst, when all the major religions of the world but one had appeared, when all the major philosophies of the world had appeared, and the world was a dreadful sink of iniquity in the Roman empire – Christ appeared and died for the ungodly.

The words "much more" are used again and again in this chapter. Paul wrote this about the death and life of Jesus: "If while we were enemies he died for us, how much more shall we be saved by his life." Then we have "how much more" repeated: "If Adam brought death on us, *how much more* can Christ bring life?" Adam's result upon me came after one trespass, but Christ's death came after millions of trespasses – yet it still worked. The contrast is drawn in so many ways.

In the 17th century, Thomas Goodwin, president of Magdalen College Oxford, said, "In God's sight there are only two men, Adam and Christ, and these two men have all other men hanging to their girdle strings." Forget the poetic language, in God's sight there are only two men, and they have all other people "in" them. You are either "in" Adam, in which case death is your king and you are fighting a losing battle with death, or "in Christ" life is yours. As I have pointed out, people object to that fact and say, "I'm quite sure that Adam's single act can't bring death in the whole human race." I say, "If you believe that, and if you deny that Adam's one act of disobedience brought death to the whole human race, then in the same breath you have denied the possibility of one man's act of righteousness giving you life – the two go together. If, on the other hand, you see that one act of sin brought death to an entire humanity that was in that man, so that when he sinned, all men sinned, and therefore death spread to all men, then you have answered the question, "How can the cross save you today?" because in exactly the same way, one man's act of righteousness, one man's obedience – perfect obedience even unto death – can bring you life, because God will accept that. You are either viewed from God's heaven as being in Adam, in which case you die forever, or you are viewed as being in Christ, in which case his one act gives you life forever.

So unless Christ comes back first, you and I are going to die – we shall all die, and that is because of what Adam did. If you accept that is the case, then you can understand that because of what one man, Jesus, did the whole human race was involved: "as in Adam all die..." and we are all born in Adam. We all were in Adam. We are all descended from his genes. As in Adam, all die, so all in Christ will be made alive. That is made possible by this corporate nature of humanity.

That is why Paul's ambition was to see one new man in Christ Jesus – not a lot of people in Christ Jesus but one new humanity, one new race. When I became a Christian I became *homo novus*, which means new man. In Christ we have become one new humanity. Death reigned over the old humanity and still does – over the finest brains and bodies and lives, death hangs, and we leave everything behind. It was asked of one of the richest men in the world, "How much did he leave?" – and the laconic reply was "Everything." The tragedy is that the greatest brains rot in the grave. That is not a natural thing. We rebel against it. It doesn't seem right that it should happen. We hate it. We put it off. We postpone it because death is the last enemy that we face.

My body is still *homo sapiens*, but I am the new man in Christ. It is a new humanity in which we belong to each

other corporately. We are not just individuals, and we see
that expanded later in the epistle.

4. SANCTIFICATION

ROMANS 6–8

A DEATH IN THE FLESH (6:1-7:25)
   1. LICENCE - Gentiles (6:1-23)
      a. Dead to sin - alive to God (1-14)
         i. Crucifixion
         ii. Resurrection
      b. Free from sin - bound to God (15-23)
         i. Then: Slaves of sin (wages of death)
         ii. Now: Slaves of righteousness (gift of life)
   2. LEGALISM - Jews (7:1-25)
      a. Dead to the law (1-6)
         i. Marriage's links
         ii. Moses' law
      b. Living under the law (7-25)
         i. Pre-conversion
         ii. Post-conversion

B LIFE IN THE SPIRIT (8:1-29)
   1. FREEDOM (1-17)
      a. Condemnation (1-4)
      b. Contrast (5-8)
      c. Conditions (9-17)
   2. FRUSTRATION (18-27)
      a. Liberation (18-22)
      b. Adoption (23-25)
      c. Intercession (26-27)
   3. FEARLESSNESS (28-39)
      a. All things helpful (28-30)
      b. All enemies silenced (31-36)
      c. All powers helpless (37-39)

PLEASE READ ROMANS 6–8

In Romans 6–8 there are certain assumptions about salvation and we need to make sure we have these assumptions right before we go any further. They will explain a lot in these chapters, but there are many different ideas about salvation that are running around the world. The first thing you need to know is that salvation is a process. It is a journey. It takes time. It takes a lifetime. It is not done in a moment, or, to put it as simply as I can, salvation is not a vertical line that you can cross with one step, from being unsaved to saved. That is a very popular idea, but the New Testament is not based on that vertical line which you can cross in one step. It is based on a horizontal line of many steps. This makes a huge difference to your thinking. You are not saved the day you are converted. You begin to be saved on that day. You start walking on the journey.

The person who made this most clear was John Bunyan, who in prison had a dream, and the dream became a book called *The Pilgrim's Progress*. In that journey, Pilgrim walks for a long way and has many different adventures on that way. From beginning the way of salvation to arriving in heaven is a long journey with many steps. That is why the New Testament calls Christianity "the Way", which means the road, the journey. It is the way of salvation that we need to have firmly in our minds. There are three phases on that journey. There is the beginning, which we call *justification*, when we are free from the penalty of past sins. Then there is *sanctification*, which is most of the journey, as we are set free from the power of sin. The goal of the journey is *glorification*, when we are set free from the presence of sin. Only then are you fully saved.

The New Testament uses the verb "save" in the three tenses: past, present, future. You have been saved; you are being saved and you will be saved. The majority of New Testament references to salvation refer to the future which none of us have yet reached. I am not saved yet, but I am on the way of salvation, taking many steps towards the goal of the salvation that is to be revealed at the last day. That is the first way of thinking we need to get hold of. If I were to ask you if you are saved, I wonder what answer you would give. I sometimes ask a group of Christians that question, and invite them to put up their hands. I also ask: "Do you believe that baptism in water is essential for salvation?" Some of them do. If you are thinking of salvation as a vertical line that you cross in one step, baptism will not be part of your thinking about salvation, but if you think of it horizontally as a journey of many steps, baptism is part of that journey, and you need it for sanctification. You need it for the journey.

The steps of *repenting toward God*, *believing in Jesus*, *being baptised in water* and *receiving the Holy Spirit* are the first four steps on the horizontal journey. All are essential for salvation. If you are thinking vertically, two of those no longer are essential for salvation in your thinking – baptism in water and baptism in the Spirit become optional extras for later. But once you think in the horizontal way about "the Way", then baptism in water and the reception of the Holy Spirit become essential for the rest of the journey. Therefore they are essential for salvation. So it makes a huge difference to your practice and behaviour as well as to your thinking.

The second thing about salvation that I want to make clear is that the journey can be slowed up and even stopped altogether. Now some people who think vertically say, "Can you lose your salvation?" When you think horizontally, you don't think you have got all salvation yet. You are on the way, and you are on a journey. You can slow up your walking. You can stop walking, and you can even walk backwards. We call it backsliding. It is actually back-walking, and you are going the wrong way so you can walk backwards. You don't lose the whole salvation, but you lose the bit you have got already. If somebody says, "Can you lose your salvation?" they're thinking, "Saved/unsaved." But you can stop the journey; you can go backwards on the journey, and you can lose all that you began with. It is just a different way of thinking.

Again, read *The Pilgrim's Progress*. At the very end of the journey, when they are at the edge of the Jordan River and Pilgrim sees the heavenly city, the other side of the Jordan, which is death, his friend says, "I'm not going through the river." He turns aside and walks down a side path, hoping there is another way to the heavenly city. Bunyan writes, "And in my dream, I saw that there is a road to hell even at the gates of heaven." He knew that at any point along the journey you can fall out of grace. You can go down a side road and get lost instead of continuing on the way of salvation. Peter has the most extraordinary thing to say about those who have begun the Way and get lost further down the road. We need to take very careful note of that. He says, "They would have been better off if they had never known the way of salvation than to start the journey and not finish it."

The third point to make is that there are two forces pulling on you – one is pulling you forwards, and the other is pulling you to go back, and you are in between those two. Christianity is a struggle, an effort. I wish somebody had told me that when I became a Christian. I would have been prepared then. Only by the grace of God can you go forward and not be pulled back. Through these three chaptes we read about the struggle between the pull of the flesh and the pull of the Spirit. The Spirit will pull you forward, but the flesh will pull you back.

There are different ways the flesh and the Spirit can pull

you. The flesh is our old self. The trouble is that when you become a Christian you don't immediately go to heaven. You have to go on living in a sad, sick, sinful, fallen world. Your body is still part of that world. Therefore the senses of your body can still pull you backwards into that world from which you came. All your senses can be grounds of temptation to go back and not forward: your sight, sound, smell, touch and taste. All the five senses of your body will be the sources of temptation to you to go back. For example, the lust of the eyes, what you see, can turn you round and pull you backwards.

That word "flesh" is very significant. Your body is still part of the old world so its habits remain after you become a Christian and must be overcome. You are not so much a person now as a civil war. It is a struggle, and an effort that needs to be made. That is why the Bible says, "Make every effort to attain that holiness without which no one will see the Lord." Sanctification is as necessary to salvation as justification, but ever since the Protestant Reformation, when Martin Luther rediscovered justification by faith, most Protestants think that is all we need for salvation. Therefore they think of that vertical line called justification. Once you are across that line, they think you are saved – if you die tonight you will go to heaven, and that's it. That is the kind of evangelism you will hear all over the world today, but it is not New Testament evangelism.

For Paul, pressing on was as important as starting the journey. That is why he said, "Forgetting the things that are behind, I stretch forward to the things that lie ahead. I'm going for the prize of that high calling of God in Christ Jesus. I'm running for it. I want to finish the race." He didn't say, "I've crossed the line. I made a decision thirty years ago and I'm safe." Most people want to be safe, but really we need to want to be saved – fully saved. The bit of me that you can see is not saved yet. It is going to be. The last part of my salvation will be the redemption of my body. We read about that in chapter 8. That is when I will be fully saved and all of me is set free from the presence of sin at last. That is when I am going to shout, "Once saved, always saved!" – because I will be once saved at last. Now that is a different way of thinking from that of many evangelicals, and different from many evangelists and preachers, but it is the way Paul thinks, and for me that is the way I am going to think. It is the apostolic gospel of salvation.

So that is the problem: my body is still in this world, and my body is part of it. The habits that were built up in the days of sin remain and pull and are there to be overcome. They can be overcome but only by the power of the Spirit. That is why I think that to tell a new convert to believe in Jesus and not to introduce them to the power of the Spirit is cruel. It is putting them on the journey and not telling them how to keep going. Baptism in water deals with your past, but it doesn't help your future. It will wash away and bury the past; it will finish the old life if you understand what it is all about, but it won't help you to keep going in the future. For that you need the baptism in the Spirit to help you to keep running.

All that may be news to you, but it lies behind and underneath chapters 6–8. Paul is now writing about Christians who can choose to walk according to the flesh or to walk according to the Spirit. One of the things I look forward to in dying is that my body will be finished with, and my senses will not be able to tempt me. You can wave a fat cheque above a dead financier's face and he won't respond at all. You cannot tempt a corpse. Someone who is dead is finished with the law as well as with sin and with temptation. It is the problem of living in a world of sin with a body that can see and hear it all that pulls me back. Now are

113

you beginning to understand the question of sanctification? *That is as necessary to get to heaven as your justification.*

In fact, without salvation including sanctification, you are not fit to go into a new universe. For the reason why God saves us from our sins, from the penalty, the power, and the presence of sin, is to make us fit to go into the new creation and not spoil it. If God took us to heaven as we are, with justification only, we would very quickly spoil it for ourselves, for him and for everybody else. Are you fit for the new heaven and the new earth? No, not yet, but salvation will get you ready for that if you always keep in mind that God's goal of saving us was not just to forgive us – that is the first bit and that puts us on the right road, but the goal is to make us perfect.

There is part of my teaching that my wife finds very hard to believe, and it is when I tell her that one day her husband will be perfect. For some reason she finds that very difficult to believe! She said to me, "If I build my faith on experience, I couldn't believe it," but she said, "I'll try and build my faith on the promises of God and believe it." But I have to believe that one day my wife will be perfect. I know it is easier for me to believe that than for her to believe the other way. Nevertheless, salvation is about being made perfect, being fully restored to the image of God until there is not a trace of sin left in you anywhere.

That is why he has to save our bodies as well, because that is where the old habits and the old traces of sin remain. You can call the body the "old man" and the new inside the "new man", but there is a struggle between the new man and the old man for every Christian, a struggle between flesh and Spirit. Christianity has a lot to do with what we do with our bodies – whether the new man is controlling the old man or the old man the new man, whether the Spirit is on top of the flesh or the flesh is on top of the Spirit. Are you beginning to understand the background to chapters 6–8?

All that is in Paul's thinking and that is what he taught his converts right from the beginning. They understood that they were not saved yet, but they were on "the way". As they continued walking on that way, walking in the Spirit, they would land up at the goal of glorification. He even suggests you can run along that road and you finish up with a prize at the end of the race. Paul did not look back on his conversion for his assurance. He lived for the future – he ran for it, and he left the things that were past behind him. He ran for it and looked to Jesus, the author and finisher of our faith. Let us run the race and get rid of the sin that can hold us back, and press on, looking to Jesus. That is the appeal of my New Testament. It is not: congratulate yourself on having started. You can be pleased that you have started. Yes, that is a big step, but there are many more steps to take: walk in the Spirit; walk in the light; walk in love; walk as sons of the kingdom. The word "walk" is all the way through the New Testament. Christianity is a walk from your old life to your new life.

When Gentiles backslide they begin to license into a blatant, sinful life; when Jews go backwards they go back into legalism, for the law is the centre of a Jew's thinking. They go back into trying to get right with God by keeping the law. They are different forms of backsliding, but both are going back into their old way of life. Paul is going to use the strongest negative language in Greek to counter every attempt to go backwards. The strongest negative is that word, "Never!" Never go back into sin! Never go back into law. In Greek, it is *me genoito*, which means "not let it be". That is best translated into English by "Never!" There are some mild translations in your polite Bibles like "By no means". Paul had stronger language than that. He is saying: Never go back! Never pick up the threads of your old life again! An alcoholic knows he must never go back to touching alcohol. Christians should know they can never go back to touching sin, not after you have started on your journey. Again, I recommend that you read *The Pilgrim's Progress* – a fascinating book.

Now we have three enemies trying to hold us back: the world, the flesh and the devil, but all three will get at us through our old bodies still living in the old world through the body's five senses. The minute I die my five senses will cease to operate. Hallelujah for that – I am out of it! But while you are in it, it is the body through which you will be attacked. The world will attack you through the body and the devil will. What we do with our flesh is going to be vital to the victory that we need. So let us look at the two ways you can die again in the flesh, because death is the wages for those who live in the flesh, the old self and the old world.

We have already noted these two ways of going back into the flesh: license which the Gentiles tend to do, and legalism which the Jews tend to do. Let us take the Gentiles first. There are many misunderstandings of the word "grace", which was mentioned in the very last sentence of chapter 5. It is a lovely word, which hardly any of the other New Testament writers use. Perhaps the reason why Paul uses it so much is that he was himself such an example of God's grace – that he, a most Jewish Jew who was persecuting Christians, trying to destroy the church, should become a major slave of Jesus to the whole Gentile world was a miracle of grace.

There are three meanings of "grace" in the Christian world today. The right meaning of the word "grace" needs to be stated again and again: grace is an undeserved favour of God, a free gift from God that you couldn't earn, that you couldn't buy, and which is freely available to you. What of the two wrong meanings? First, some Christians have begun to think that grace is an irresistible force. Calvinists believe that, and therefore Presbyterians believe it, and because Presbyterian missionaries went to Indonesia, that is a bit of a problem there. Those who hold that view believe that this grace of God is so powerful that nobody can resist it, nobody can refuse it, nobody can do anything about it. The grace of God decides who gets saved, and nobody can do anything about that. Grace is such an irresistible force that it decides who goes to heaven and who goes to hell. It decides that once you start on the journey, you will finish it because it is an irresistible force. To me, that is a travesty of the scriptures.

Grace is not an irresistible force. Nor is it, at the opposite extreme, *unconditional forgiveness.* I am afraid you'll find the source for that in Singapore. This teaches that you do not need to repent to be forgiven – that it is unconditional, and that when you come to Christ all your future sins are forgiven as well as your past sins. You will never again need to confess a sin and have it forgiven. That is a teaching of "free grace", just as the second wrong meaning was called "sovereign grace". I believe that grace is the undeserved favour of God, which can be resisted and refused, but when it is accepted is one of the most lovely things in the world – the grace of our Lord Jesus Christ be with you. So bear in mind that the word "grace" has these three different meanings, two of which are very misleading, and one of which will bring you great joy and peace.

It is arguments about grace that Paul is going to deal with now, and people who take advantage of grace, those who exploit it. He deals with it in an imaginary dialogue, but I am quite sure the questions he faces have been presented to him by the people he has been dealing with. The questions always begin with the same words: What then shall we say? Then comes the question, and then Paul always begins by saying, "Never!" That explains why he has such an emphatic negative answer.

So the first question in Romans 6 is: "Shall we go on sinning that grace may increase? Shall we go on sinning because God's grace forgives that sin, and therefore my sinning will produce more grace? The more I sin, the more grace he can have for me. Jesus did say, "The more you are forgiven, the more you will love me," but he would have been horrified with this logical question. If my sinning produces God's grace then let's sin some more – let's have more grace. It is logical but it is a devilish argument. When the devil gets hold of your logical brain he can make you think all kinds of ugly things.

What is the answer to such people? Well, the first answer is your water baptism and what happened in your baptism. Unfortunately, you may have been baptised in water without realising what was happening when you were plunged into that water and lifted up again. Did you know what God was doing in that? Did you know what you were doing apart from getting wet in front of a lot of other people? It is not just a "wet witness". There is something profound that happens in water baptism. I am not talking about a sprinkling of a bit of water on a baby's forehead. I am talking about believer's baptism by immersion when you are lowered into the water, and if you were left there you would drown. It is a death. You are being buried out of sight, and then you are being raised, but there is much more to it than that. You may be baptised in water, but you are being baptised into Christ. Paul teaches that it is a profound identification with him when you were baptised. You know that you are baptised into Christ and therefore into his death. When you were lifted up again you were baptised into his resurrection and raised to a new life. How could you, after that, talk about sinning again to bring more grace into the world? It is just a total contradiction to your baptism.

Can I put it this way? When you become a Christian, you

realise that Jesus died for you and rose again for you. As you mature and understand what actually happened: you were baptised *into* him, and therefore you were crucified with him, and you were resurrected with him. That is what happened in your baptism. That is why the appeal of the New Testament is this: you have been crucified with Christ, therefore put to death the flesh. Crucify this part of you that still hangs on to the old world, and by the power of the Spirit you can do that. Every Christian should be a murderer of themselves and of their old life. You can do it. The power of the Spirit enables you to use that identification. You have not only been crucified with Christ, you have been raised with Christ, you have ascended with Christ, and you are seated with him in heavenly places. That is what's happened to you. You have been baptised into him. You weren't given your own name in baptism. You were given his name. You are now in him and therefore your baptism alone is enough to prevent you from talking about sinning again. You have been crucified to sin as he was crucified. You have been raised to a new life as he was. That is the first answer to this question.

The second answer takes it a stage further and says that what you do with your body now is going to be crucial. You can either let your body become an instrument of sin again, or you can become a body that is an instrument of righteousness. You have got the choice. Why do it – when you have been baptised and you said goodbye to your old life? I have had some wonderful experiences of baptism in water that really finished an old life. One was a young Hell's Angel who had a tattoo of the devil on his body. He was baptised into Christ and he came up out of the water minus one tattoo. The Devil was washed off his body in baptism. That happened in our own local town where I live. It was real, and if you tell him baptism is just a symbol, he will laugh at you. He will say, "Baptism got the devil off me" – off his body. That young man is now an instrument of righteousness. He is using his body the right way. Do you see the difference?

I remember emptying the pool in the church one day and there was a pipe and a pouch of tobacco sodden in the bottom of the pool. I thought, "There is somebody who's getting rid of his old life." I don't care if the baptism becomes a garbage dump, it is the best place for it. I could tell many stories of what happens in baptism. It is neither a symbol nor a "wet witness". Too many Baptists think that is all it is. "Are you willing to get dripping wet in front of everybody? Good, that's your duty to the Lord" – but it has nothing to do with that, it is going into Christ. A person who understands his or her baptism will not want to go back into sinning. A person who has buried his old life won't want to raise it up again. To summarise this point: it matters what you do with your body – don't offer it to sin, offer it to righteousness. That is how you overcome the flesh. You offer it to the right master.

We have already seen that you are now dead to sin and alive to God and that when you became a Christian you exchanged one slavery for another. Everybody in the world is a slave. We don't like that term nowadays. It is "politically incorrect", to say the least, but that is the truth. Jesus said, "If you sin, you are a slave to sin." It becomes your master. You become an addict to sin, but when you become a Christian you are exchanging that slavery for another kind. You are now bound to God. Paul doesn't hesitate to use the metaphor of slavery. We have watered that down to "service", but Paul said, "I'm a slave of Jesus." A slave has no rights of his own. He has been bought with a price. He has no money of his own, no food of his own. He is totally dependent on his Lord and Master. That is slavery. So Paul teaches that we are now to regard ourselves as slaves to God, as bound to righteousness.

Again, once you have realised that, put it into practice by reckoning it (Romans 6:11). It is interesting that Paul uses this word "reckon" as a mental exercise. Just as God now reckons you as righteous – counts you as righteous – you also must join him and reckon yourself dead, and a slave to good things. But then he adds the point that slavery to God has much better benefits than slavery to the devil. When you are a slave to God you have the free gift of eternal life. When you are a slave to sin you will get your wages, and the wages of sin is death. When you are a slave to God you get the free gift of eternal life. What a difference!

Would you rather ultimately face death or ultimately have life? Then become a slave of the Lord. You have been crucified with him. You have been raised with him. You have ascended with him. Well, become his slave. Reckon yourself bound. Reckon yourself dead. We have to do a reckoning just as God, on his part, has done a reckoning when he justified you. We need to respond to that by reckoning ourselves, by constantly thinking, "I'm dead; I'm bound. I'm someone else's slave."

Two boys in England were at the same school and really close friends, but when they left school they lost touch with each other. One found Christ and became a Baptist pastor in London. The other literally went to the devil, got on to drugs, and to crime to pay for it, and did everything wrong. At twenty-four the bad one was suicidal and was about to end his life. Then he had a thought. He said, "There was that nice boy at school. If I could find him, I'm sure he could help me," but he didn't know where he had gone to. He didn't know any better than to go to the nearest spiritist medium and ask her to tell him where his friend was. The spiritist medium actually said, "He's in the north of London and I can describe the house that he lived in." She described this house opposite a park of trees and she described the colour of the front door in detail. The young man set off from Bristol where he lived, and he searched north London for days and days until he found the house. But the medium had said to him, "I'm sorry to have to tell you, but your friend is dead." She said, "I can tell you the date he died," and she did. He found the house, and he went to the front door and rang the bell, and the door opened and there was his friend, the Baptist pastor. The boy said, "I went to a medium and she told me where you lived, but she said you were dead." He said, "Well come in and let's talk," and then the boy said, "She told me the date on which you died." He said, "What date was that?" He told him, and the Baptist pastor said, "Do you know, that was the date of my baptism?"

The spirit world knows the date of your baptism. Isn't that amazing? From your baptism onwards you are dead to sin, and you are a slave to Christ now. Tell the devil that: "I'm baptised; I'm dead; I'm buried; I'm bound to someone else now, and you can't touch me." Try it. You are not bluffing. It is the devil who bluffs. It is he whose bluff needs to be called. He can get at you through the world and your old body and its senses. Just tell him to go to hell and see what happens. I am serious. Paul is telling you to reckon yourself dead and realise then that you really are, and you will find it to be true. I have advised people to do that and they have discovered that it is right. You call the devil's bluff and he can't do anything with you. It is all there in Romans 6.

If Gentiles attempted to go back into license and the pull of their flesh, the old life drags them back. By the way, so many people have started the journey of salvation and not finished it that if we could keep them all our churches would be packed. I did some research into the last Billy Graham Crusade in London and discovered that of sixteen who went forward to his appeal only one is still walking with the Lord. That was the statistic five years later: of sixteen who went forward, one went on with the Lord. I am afraid that is true of so many crusades if we are honest, because we told them, "Take one step, say the sinner's prayer, and you're in, you're safe." They immediately assumed they had stepped across the line, whether they had been baptised or not. They had not been told, "You've started a journey, a walk in the Spirit that will land you in heaven at the end, but it's a walk. It's a pilgrim's progress." How many of those who go forward in an altar call are told that? They need to be told it will be a struggle.

The Jews, as we have noted, are tempted to go back into legalism and trying to be good enough for God by keeping the law. That is their backsliding. The word "law" now occurs twenty-four times in chapter 7 and Paul is now talking as a Jew to Jews. The word "law" is used in at least three different ways in this chapter, which can be a bit misleading when you first read it. The first point he wants to make to the Jew is that you are now dead to the law. He uses as an illustration the law of marriage and divorce. He says, "Don't you know the law about divorce and remarriage?"

I think he is quoting the divine law rather than Roman or Jewish law, because the divine law is stricter than both. Jesus told us the divine law: that if anyone divorces and remarries they are committing adultery, and, since adultery is the sin of a married person, it means that God does not recognise the divorce, and that in his sight you are still married to the first partner. Therefore, in marrying someone else you are committing adultery against your first partner. Paul says that is the law. He goes on to say if a woman or a man marries someone other than their spouse while their spouse is still alive, they are committing adultery against their married partner. That is straight talk. You know in the Western world at any rate, there are now as many divorces inside the church as outside, and remarriages. The Lord's teaching is ignored.

His law is being broken widely. Britain is now as bad as America for this inside church. Many of the evangelical leaders, national leaders in Britain, are on their second or third wife. It is accepted. Nobody is quoting the law of God. I have written a book on that, entitled *Remarriage is Adultery, Unless....*

Marriage here is an illustration. The moment your spouse has died you are totally free to marry someone else. I have conducted a number of beautiful second marriages within months of a wife dying. One was a Baptist pastor and his wife who said as she died, "You won't be any good on your own, you need a woman to look after you, so marry this lady" – who was the great Spurgeon's granddaughter. I married them two months after the wife died and they were blissfully happy. He was free to. Death ends marriage. Nothing else does in God's sight. Therefore Paul says, "You can see that the law does not apply to the dead." When you are dead, you are free from the law, and he immediately goes on to talk about Moses' law, which is the same as marriage law. When you died with Christ, you died to the law. You are finished with the law of Moses. Thank God for that! There are 613 of them, and most of them I couldn't keep. I remember challenging three rabbis. I accused them all of not keeping Moses' law, and they were furious. I quoted laws to them and they said, "Oh well, we can't keep that now. We have no temple," and, "Oh well, the chief rabbi allows us to do this instead." All three of them made excuses for the fact they didn't keep Moses' law. I remember one of them looked at me and said, "What are you? Are you reformed or Orthodox?" They thought I was Jewish. I think the nose misled them a bit! Finally he said to me, "I know who you are. You're a Christian, and you think you're not under Moses' law, don't you?"

"Yes," I said, "and you don't know what a relief that is!"

We had quite a conversation. That was on a plane, and I had only got on it because I had the staff seat facing backwards, where the cabin steward sits for landing. I had managed to get it cheaply to get to Israel on that occasion, but that is another story.

I don't have to keep Moses' law, not even the Ten Commandments. Some of them are repeated in the new covenant, and those bind me, but I am not bound by the Sabbath law. I am not bound by the tithing law. I am astonished how many pastors teach tithing. It belongs to the old covenant. I do teach giving, not tithing. That was a tax for the Jews. The Sabbath was a tax on their time, and tithing is a tax on their income. God doesn't tax under the new covenant. He loves a cheerful giver, and that does not mean grinning when the collection plate passes, it means someone who is giving because he wants to. Under the new covenant, God doesn't want your money if you don't want to give it, but if you really understand grace you will want to give far more than a tithe. For some people in our churches today (unmarried single mothers and so on) a tithe is far too much for them, but for the average Christian today a tithe is far too little. Teach new covenant giving, don't impose the legalism of Moses' law on people. We are under the law of Christ. We are under the law of the Spirit. We are under the new covenant with the law written on our hearts rather than on tablets of stone outside us.

So the basic argument Paul uses here is what he uses with Gentiles on license: you have been crucified with Christ and you have been raised with Christ – you are now dead to the law. You are married to God. You have got a new partner. You are bound to God. The old life with its sinful passions is finished. The new life has begun – a life in the Spirit, a life of service to God and others. Then, in 7:7–25, he writes about living under the law. There is a great controversy about this passage. Is he talking as a Christian, or is he describing his pre-Christian days? It is a very personal part of the letter. The word "I" occurs so often. Forty-four times he says, "I", "me" and "my" in just a few verses. It is too real not to be his own experience.

"Oh, wretched man that I am! Who will deliver me?" That is a cry of the heart. It has got to be real, but is he reliving his days before conversion or his days afterwards? Is this the kind of struggle that he had before he knew Christ or the kind of struggle that a Christian can have? I have books on my shelves of theologians arguing those two cases. I believe it is both. The first section (vv. 7–13) is in the past tense and clearly refers to Paul's pre-Christian days. In vv. 14–25 I think he is describing his Christian days, because there he says, "My mind accepts the law of God and my mind wants to serve God and wants to live according to his law, but my members have a law that doesn't." I believe he is describing the kind of tension a Christian can get into when he is trying to do it by himself. So then he says, "I myself serve the law," but then, as in Galatians: "But the life I now live, I don't live any more. It's not me."

So I am going to divide this section into two. First there are the pre-conversion days (in the past tense; 7–13) – the law made him sin. The law aroused sin. He did not know the sin of coveting until the law said, "You shall not do it." In fact, you know perfectly well that to say something negative to a person is to make them want to do it more than ever. "Don't touch that!" – you want to touch it! I was discussing business methods with my adviser. If you take a negative line with businessmen they react negatively, but if you put it positively, they will react positively. There are a lot of negatives in the law. "You shall not" is more frequent than "You shall". There was nothing wrong with the law. Paul teaches that it was good, wholesome and holy. It was God's law, but there is something wrong with me that when I am told not to do a thing I want to do it.

I remember a boy in the RAF who said to me, "You don't believe that story about the garden of Eden, do you Padre?"

I replied, "Let me tell you another story. I'm going to put you into a library with thousands of books on every subject you're interested in and I'm going to leave you alone in the library and shut the door. Then you notice that there's one book on the top shelf with *Not to be Read by Anyone under 21* on the cover. (He was nineteen.) I said, "I'm going to leave you in that library for as long as you like. You can spend a lifetime reading every interesting book on every subject, but don't touch that book."

Then he said, "Oh, I'll believe the story of the garden of Eden now."

It is human nature. "Don't touch." What does it feel like? Why shouldn't I touch it? That is what the law does to people, not because it is a bad law, but because a good law makes bad people do that.

So for Paul in his pre-conversion days, as a Jew trying to keep the law, he found it simply aroused sin in him, made him want to do it. He confessed that the one law he could never keep was "Thou shalt not covet." The Pharisees (and he was a Pharisee) were notoriously greedy people. When they were told not to covet, they coveted. The law brought sin to Paul in his pre-conversion days but not because the law was sin. He begins the section with a question, "What then shall we say? Is the law sin? Never!" There it is again. The law was holy and good – God's law, his holiness law – but bad people cannot keep it and are stimulated to disobey it when they are told not to do certain things.

That was Paul's pre-Christian days, but when you come to vv. 14–25 he must be a Christian now. His mind has changed. His mind does not want to break the law. His mind accepts the law of God. His mind wants to do good, but he finally just can't help doing evil. "It's because," he says, "there are two laws. There's God's law in my mind but there's another law in my members." That is the law of sin. It is the same problem. It obviously had been a crisis in his personal Christian life when the big "I" took over – and "I", myself that wanted to do good, found it impossible to avoid evil. He is describing that Christian experience. He finishes up by saying, "Who will get me out of this tension?" Immediately, he gives the answer: I thank God there is a way out, and there is a deliverance. Who shall deliver me from this tension? I thank God through Jesus there is a way out of it. That leads into the whole of chapter 8, which tells you the way out of struggling between the flesh and the Spirit.

Life in the Spirit; death in the flesh either through license or legalism – either will produce the wages of death, but now we turn to life in the Spirit. We come out from under the clouds into the sunshine of chapter 8. Again, remember there were no chapter and verse divisions in Paul's letter. He goes straight on from the struggle of chapter 7, from which he needs to be delivered, to write about the deliverance, and he thanks God for it. There are three things characteristic of life in the Spirit: freedom, frustration and fearlessness.

First there is freedom – "The law of the Spirit of life has set me free from the law of sin and death." In other words, I will never get out of that struggle, but the Spirit will set me free. The two chapters must be read together, because what the law could not do, God did through sending his Son in the likeness of sinful flesh. Many Christians have missed that phrase, but it tells us that Christ was born with sinful flesh. He inherited that through his mother. Now think that through. The Catholics teach that Mary, the mother, was immaculate. Her immaculate conception of Jesus defied normal physical inheritance laws. Jesus was born without sinful flesh because Mary had been. Well I cannot find that anywhere in the Bible, but I find that Protestants think Jesus had an immaculate conception, but he was born of Mary, and she was born with sinful flesh. That word "likeness" (of sinful flesh) has thrown some people off balance. It is the same word that he has used in Philippians 2 where it says Jesus took on the likeness of man. It is not just the appearance of man, it means the exact reproduction.

I am thankful that Jesus had to fight the battles I have to fight. I have to fight the battles with the world, the flesh, and the Devil. If you believe Jesus had an immaculate conception, he did not have to fight the flesh, so he did not have to fight my battle. He inherited that from his mother, and he overcame it. He overcame the world; he overcame the devil and he overcame the flesh. Praise you Jesus! You were the victor over every enemy that I have, and you overcame them all. He never sinned. Now there is something quite profound for you to think over. He was born in the likeness of sinful flesh, and he never sinned – amazing! That means he can help me with my flesh. He can help me with all my temptations because he has been tempted in all points, just as we are. Most of our temptations come from the flesh. He had them, and he overcame them. He can help you to do the same. Hallelujah for that!

So we recall that we have the choice in Christ: with his Spirit in us we can either walk according to the flesh or according to the Spirit. That choice has to be made every day in life and every step of the way on the journey of salvation. Every single decision we make, we can make according to the flesh or according to the Spirit. Unbelievers cannot make that choice. They don't have the Spirit. They have to choose everything according to the flesh, according to this old world, and their body matches their Spirit. They all belong to the world, but we have the choice and we can decide every morning when we get up: "I'm going to walk in the Spirit today", or, "I'm going to walk in the flesh today." So first there's no condemnation to those who are in the Spirit because Jesus took the condemnation for us. Jesus came in our sinful flesh and overcame it and died in the flesh too, and can therefore conquer it in us and give us a choice.

Therefore, 8:9–17 gives the conditions of that choice. There is one word that occurs six times in that passage, namely the word "if". *If* we live by the flesh – this is what will happen. *If* we live by the Spirit – this is what will happen. There is a big "if" about the Christian life. It even says, "If the Spirit dwells in you". If he doesn't, then you don't even belong. That is v. 8. *If* you are controlled by the flesh, this is what happens; *if* you are led by the Spirit, this is what will result. He goes right through and gives us many examples of what happens if we do one or the other. If we walk in the Spirit we will be led by the Spirit, and instinctively will shout out, "Abba, Father!" We will have that kind of relationship, if we walk in the Spirit – we will recognise God like a little child recognising its parent. It says we will be led by the Spirit. If you walk in the flesh you won't be led by the Spirit, but if you walk in the Spirit you will be led by the Spirit because we are sons of God. If we are sons of God, Paul says, we shall be heirs of God. We shall inherit all that God has. We shall be the main legatees of God's will. There are conditions, and I leave you to go through it carefully for yourself. The final big "if" is: *if* we share his sufferings, we shall share his glory. To try to avoid suffering is to try to avoid the glory. Go through all the instances of "if" in that passage and see how you measure up.

The next thing is *frustration*. What a strange thing to put about life in the Spirit! Surely in life in the Spirit we are free? We should be relaxed about everything. We should have no worries, but in fact, when you walk in the Spirit you will be frustrated. The more you walk in the Spirit the more frustrated you will get. Why? Because we are still living in a sinful, sad world and not only human nature is fallen around us, but nature itself is fallen. The creation has fallen. Sin has not only affected human beings. There is "nature, red in tooth and claw", as an English poet put it. You can see evidence for that everywhere you look. Nature is cruel. It is at war. Darwin said it is a struggle for survival between the fittest species and the not-so-fit species. Everywhere he looked in nature he saw this struggle going on. Creation reflects our frustration.

What is that frustration? Very simply, we long to be in the new universe. We know it is coming and we are frustrated because we can't live in it yet. We long for that day when we are fully liberated as sons of God. That is the day we get our new bodies. Interestingly enough, nature itself is groaning for that day when we get our new bodies, for what will follow is a transformed nature. You read about it in Isaiah. Nature itself is going to be redeemed. Christ is not stopping with redeeming people, he is going to redeem all things and all things will be made new. There is a new universe coming, a whole new world for us to live in. This world is groaning and travailing. Somehow, every earthquake and tremor reminds me of that, when the earth groans and struggles. I can tell you now that there will be no earthquakes in the new earth. It is going to be quite different. You groan when you are frustrated, when you want to be somewhere else and not here. So we are groaning and nature is groaning, and it is all building up to a day when all things will be made new. We are caught up in a cosmic frustration which will be relieved by the liberation of the sons of God.

Not only is creation around us groaning, but creation within us groans too. It infects our prayer life. There are times when we are not sure what we ought to pray about.

There are times when we are so frustrated with things as they are that we don't know how to put it into words. Don't worry, the Holy Spirit will intercede for you. Pray in tongues; pray in the Spirit; let the Spirit pray on your behalf. Let the frustration out in this way. Don't get all tied up in knots yourself about it, but let it out. Let the Holy Spirit take over your prayer life and intercede for you.

There is something very deep in this section in this letter of Paul. He is putting the whole thing on a cosmic base. We are getting a very big canvas now, aren't we? From just an individual being filled with the Spirit and praying in tongues, we are now looking at a whole creation that is groaning and the Christians in it that are groaning with the same frustration, longing for the future, wondering how and when to pray for it. Our adoption as sons will come when we get our new bodies and all of us is saved.

We are the only people in the world who believe that we will get a new body for ourselves. It is totally different from the doctrine of reincarnation, because all doctrines of reincarnation that you find in other religions tell you that you will come back as someone else, either a better or a worse person than you are now. You will come back as someone else or, as the old song puts it, "A duck could be somebody's mother." You can come back as an animal in reincarnation. I have no ambition to be a duck, but I'm getting a new body for John David Pawson, and I will know it is me. That is my reincarnation. It is a reincarnation, which means to be re-embodied, but it is my body I'll come back in – not yours, not somebody else's.

That is the heart of the Christian faith: *I believe in the resurrection of the body*. Nobody else did in those days. They believed in the immortality of the soul – that when you died it was like taking a glass of water, smashing the glass, and letting the water go into the sea. That was the Greek concept of death. The water would lose all its identity in the sea. The body would be broken, finished with. The soul would go sailing on, but not with any identity, just as part of the universe. There is no hope in that, and it was against all that background the Christians said, "We believe in the resurrection of the body." A new body for a new world; don't let the Jehovah's Witnesses get away with all the talk of the new world. We believe in it, and we are looking forward to it.

We have thought about the liberation that is coming, the adoption which will be complete when we get new bodies, and the intercession of the Spirit who helps us even now in our frustration. The other thing that life in the Spirit brings is *fearlessness*. The God who is now in control of our lives is responsible for us, and in three ways we have courage to face whatever comes. First, *all things will be helpful to us*. God will make all things work together for good to those who love him and are called according to his purpose, so whatever happens to you will do you good. Isn't that a great thought? He will make all things helpful to you.

The next thing is that *all your accusers will be silent*. Who will bring any charge, against God's chosen people? Who can accuse us? Nobody – God will silence every accusation against us. So every circumstance will help us, every accuser will be silenced and, finally, *all the powers will be helpless* to separate you from the love of God in Christ Jesus. Notice the word "all" that I have put in for those three things: all things helpful; all accusers silent, and all powers helpless. "For I am persuaded," says Paul, "that neither death, nor life, nor angels, nor principalities, nor powers, nor things present, nor things to come, nor height, nor depth, nor any other creature shall be able to separate us from the love of God in Christ Jesus."

It is no wonder Christians have seized on that verse as one of the most comforting verses in the Bible. It is a wonderful verse. I just want you to notice there is one thing missing from that list, and that is *you*. No other creature will have the power to separate you from God, but you have that power. In the next few chapters we are going to see the possibility of that, but nothing else in all creation will be able to cut between you and your God. That is a wonderful promise! Seize it! Hold it! The chapter begins with no condemnation and it ends with no separation. We live between the two and that is a wonderful place to live.

5. ISRAEL

ROMANS 9–11

A SELECTED IN THE PAST (9:1-29)
    1. Paul's sorrow (1-5)
        a. His anguish
        b. Their advantages
    2. God's sovereignty (6-29)
        a. His remnant
            i. Not everyone
            ii. Not eldest
        b. His right
            i. His righteousness?
            ii. Our responsibility?
        c. His reason
            i. Justice and mercy
            ii. Jews and Gentiles

B STUMBLING IN THE PRESENT (9:30-10:21)
    1. Failure to achieve righteousness (9:30-10:13)
        a. Works of the law
        b. Faith in the Lord
    2. Failure to receive revelation (10:14-21)
        a. Heard but not heeded
        b. Understood but not undertaken

C SAVED IN THE FUTURE (11:1-32)
    1. Past – some Jews (1-10)
        a. Remnant held
        b. Rest hardened
    2. Present – many Gentiles (11-24)
        a. Good – making Jews jealous
        b. Bad – making Gentiles arrogant
    3. Future – all Israel (25-32)
        a. Softened heart
        b. Shared mercy

DOXOLOGY (11:33-36)
    God is inscrutable   )
           independent   ) to Him be glory
           indispensable   )

PLEASE READ ROMANS 9–11

In Romans 9–11 we have reached the heart of the letter and the reason for it. These three chapters are all about Israel. Israel is in the New Testament as well as the Old. Over seventy times the word "Israel" appears in your New Testament and it always has an ethnic meaning. It means the Jewish people every time. In these three chapters we have Israel mentioned twenty-nine times. It is not a parenthesis. Too many commentaries say that Paul is off on one of his own ideas here and that it is not essential to understand Romans by including these chapters. As we have noted, there were no chapter divisions in Paul's letter, and it all flows straight on so beautifully.

At the end of chapter eight we had that magnificent statement that nothing can separate us from God. The obvious question immediately comes: well, what about the Jews? Are they not separated from God now? The answer is: Never! It is that same, strong negative, but too many Christians in the church today have dismissed Israel and think that the church is the new Israel. Have you heard that phrase? You won't find it in your Bible. Israel is still Israel. They are still God's people. He is still their God. He will keep the covenant promises he made to them and is doing so before our very eyes. In our day we are seeing the promises to Israel fulfilled. Not totally – they are not all back in the land. Only half of them are back, but I am waiting to see God bring the other half back. They only have a quarter of the land God promised them, but I am waiting to see the other three-quarters given to them.

God has a lot to do yet with Israel which he promised to do, and it will take some time to be done. So don't talk as if all Israel is back in the land. Sadly, if they won't come voluntarily, he raises the forces of anti-Semitism to hurry them up. Anti-Semitism is growing in my country, in America, and in many European countries. God is saying, "Come back; come back." When I get the privilege of speaking in a synagogue I tell them, "God wants you back in the land." Of course, too many of them are in business elsewhere and have their resources elsewhere, and they are not going to leave until it is really impossible to stay and be a Jew. Why did I mention all that? I don't know, except that Israel always means the Jewish people. It is never applied to the church. There is one possible exception to that in Galatians, but when you examine it closely it is not an exception. There is no reason at all to say that the church is the new Israel. What we will find out in these chapters is that the church has been grafted on the tree called Israel. We are now fellow citizens with them in the commonwealth of Israel, but the word Israel still and always will mean God's chosen people, the Jews.

Now in these three chapters, we have three main statements made about them. Number one: in the past they were *selected*, chosen from among other people. We will look at that in detail. In the second chapter (not quite corresponding to the chapter divisions), in the present they are *stubborn*. They are stumbling over Christ who is the rock on which they were meant to stand, but they are falling over him. Finally, chapter 11 brings us a mystery. The word "mystery" in the New Testament never means something difficult to understand or something incomprehensible. It means something that we could never have discovered by ourselves, but which God has revealed. It is a secret that he kept and has now shared with us. That secret is that one day all Israel will be saved. We shall look at what that means, who it means, and what it actually means to be saved. There are the three major headlines for our study now, and they roughly correspond to the three chapters. Whoever divided the chapters didn't get it quite right.

Let us look at the past. Israel are God's chosen people. He selected them and Paul begins by stating it was a daily sorrow to him. He had the joy of the Holy Spirit but at the same time, he had a deep sorrow in his heart that he had to live with: that his own people, the Jewish people, had not seen the truth that God had shown them in Christ. That is a very heavy burden for a man like Paul to have to carry. He is being honest. He calls the Father, the Son and the Holy Spirit to witness that he is telling the truth. He says, "I have a daily agony, an anguish that my relatives, my own race, my nearest and dearest, should not be sharing the good news that I preach." Consider what advantages they had over every other nation on earth, what a lot God invested in them. Then to have them, as a nation, not accepting his greatest gift – that would be a pain in God's heart, but it is very much a pain that Paul has. He even says, "I could wish myself cursed for their sake if it would save them." Now I don't know that I could ever say that. Could you? Would you be willing to go to hell if it would get your family to heaven? I am not sure I have got that kind of feeling, but Paul says, "I could wish myself in hell if it would get my people into heaven." Amazing statement, and he has just called on God to testify as a witness to his honesty in saying this, but he tells us that. Actually, it was Christ who said that of the world, and Christ wished himself cursed to get us all to heaven. Paul is sharing Christ's agony of heart. He said, "I could wish the same." Fortunately, God would not let him do that, but he is just telling us how deep his feelings are for his own race.

Now he lists their advantages. They were adopted as sons of God. They had the divine glory in their own temple. They had the covenants of God. Every covenant in scripture was made with the Jewish people. The covenant with Noah was with their ancestor. The covenant with Abraham was with their father. The covenant with Moses was with them. The covenant with David was with them, and the new covenant, says Jeremiah, will be made with the house of Israel and the house of Judah. Never forget that. The new covenant was first promised to the Jewish people. When Jesus, on the night before he died, said, "This is my blood of the new covenant," it was for the Jewish people first. Remember that. They received the law. They had temple worship. All the promises of God in the Old Testament were made to them. The patriarchs were theirs and, above all, it was to them that God gave his Son, the Messiah, the Christ.

There is a bit of division now among scholars about the next phrase. "They were the human ancestors of Christ," and then it says, "who is God over all." Some people have really said that is going too far to say that Jesus is God, but I believe that is the right reading. Those who have taken another reading I think just could not cope with that statement. That was the climax of the advantage of the Jewish people. They gave us Jesus, and we should always be grateful to the Jewish people, to that couple, Joseph and Mary, who were probably in their late teens when Jesus was born. They kept him safe from Herod and they took him as a refugee to Egypt. Are you grateful to Joseph and Mary for doing that? Unless they had looked after Jesus we would not have a Saviour. The Jews were God's chosen people.

So he goes on from his own sorrow to God's sovereignty in that, and says God has the right to choose whoever he wants to use. That is surely true. God doesn't choose people according to human ideas, because everybody would have expected in each case that the patriarch's eldest son would inherit the promise of God, but in every case God chose the younger son quite deliberately. He chose Jacob, not Esau, and Esau had been the first of the twins to be born. He chose Isaac, not Ishmael, so he did not follow the normal routine of the eldest son being the heir of the family. God has the liberty to choose whom he will, and he still does. I want to emphasise one very important thing about the choice of God here. He was not choosing them for salvation, he was choosing them for his service. That is so important because Calvinists have read too much into this chapter – that salvation is a matter entirely for God to choose whom he wants to save. That is not the teaching in this chapter. God has the liberty to choose whom he wants to serve a purpose, and that is the real heart of his election in this passage. He chose the Jewish people for a purpose. He wanted to reach the whole world. I have told you already about the "scandal of particularity", as the philosophers call it. Why did he choose one people to give his revelation to the rest? Well, that was his choice. You can argue about it and say he should have chosen other nations as well, but he didn't. "How odd of God to choose the Jews...." Therefore we have to go to the Jewish people if we want to find God. It is the only channel of his revelation to the whole world. That is why he chose them.

At this point Paul has to face a question. The question is this: It looks as if God has made a mistake, doesn't it? It looks as if his whole choice was wrong. He chose the wrong people because they have not followed it through. They have rejected their own Messiah. But surely God wouldn't make such a big mistake. Those who believe that he did make a mistake in choosing the Jews go on to say that is why he chose the church to replace them. That is not true at all. He did not make a mistake. His promises have not failed, but we have to accept that the explanation is that not all the sons of Jacob are Israel. In other words, God chose the Jews to be his channel to the world and there have always been some

Jews who were faithful – a remnant, if you like. Maybe many of them were not faithful, but some of them were. It was through the faithful remnant that God's choice was justified and his purpose fulfilled.

When Jesus chose twelve apostles, he chose twelve Jewish men, and that is how the church began. They did not fail him. One of the extraordinary things about Jesus' birth that I never cease to be amazed at is that he was the only person in the whole of history who chose to be born. You did not choose to be born. I did not choose to be born. You did not choose your parents and I did not choose mine. He was the only human being who ever lived who chose to be born and chose his own parents. Amazing, but he chose Jewish parents, and he it was who decided to be born of Mary, not of Joseph. He had another Father, but he chose Mary as his mother. God was his Father, and in that unique, miraculous birth, with a divine Father and a Jewish mother, came together the full humanity and divinity of our Lord.

As long as God had a remnant of the Jews to work through, he had all he needed for his purpose. Not all Jacob's descendants are Israel, but those who were God's Israel, God's true faithful people, played a crucial role all the way through scripture right up to Simeon and Anna, who welcomed Christ's birth. There was always the remnant, and Paul says in Romans 11: "and there still is" – and always will be. There will always be Jewish people who are faithful to God, however small a remnant. It is through them that God fulfils his purpose.

So the first point I want to make is about his *remnant*. It was not every Jew and it was not the eldest of the family. It was clearly God's choice. Think of King David. When the prophet Samuel went to visit Jesse, Jesse had a number of boys, and he brought them before Samuel one by one because he knew Samuel was here to choose the next king.

Samuel said, "No, it's not that one; no, not that one," and all of them came and went. Samuel had to say, "Have you no more boys? Because I'm sure God sent me to this house to find a boy." "Oh well," he said, "We've got the youngest, but he's out looking after the sheep." Samuel said, "Bring him here." As soon as he saw him, he said, "This is the boy!" It was the last one Jesse would have chosen and was the last one, but it was God's choice. God's choice is very particular and very different from man's choice. When Israel wanted to choose their first king, they chose a tall, handsome man who stood head and shoulders above everybody else and they thought, "We've got a real king now." What a mistake they made! He may have been head and shoulders above people physically, but he was a little man spiritually, who finished up consulting mediums.

So the remnant – there always has been and always will be a minority of Jews whom God can use. Do you know that in the history of the church for two thousand years there have always been some believing Jews in the church? Of course it was started by Jews. Surprising choice – the point that Paul wants to make here is that is God's right to choose, and to question his choice and his way of working is sheer cheek. It is impudence for the clay to say to the potter, "What are you doing?" He is the sovereign God, and God has rights. We are so busy talking about our rights now – Declaration of Human Rights, document U222 in the United Nations – we are always writing about our rights, but nobody seems to be talking about God's rights. He made us. He has a right over us and he has a right to choose whom he will.

The interesting thing is when you look around a congregation he does not choose a lot of the top people. He does choose a few, but most of God's people are people that the world would not choose to be influential for God, ordinary people. God chose us and used us – amazing! That is his choice. He loves to take a "nobody" and turn them into a somebody because he will get the glory then. If you are a great and noble and rich person you could get the glory for what you do, but God wants the glory. So he chooses those who have nothing and he makes them somebody. That is his right. If we start saying that God is unjust we are questioning his will and we are being very cheeky. God has his reason, and here we come to the heart of this matter of election.

God does not pick people out of a hat. He doesn't get a telephone directory and then put a finger on a page and say, "Right, I'll choose him." He has reasons for his choice, and he has reasons for choosing some for his mercy and some for his justice. He has a reason to choose this person to be an example of his mercy and that person to be an example of his judgment. There is a little phrase that Paul slips in here that explains the reason why he chooses a Pharaoh to be an example of his judgment and a Moses to be an example of his mercy. Why did he choose Pharaoh? Paul says it was his right to choose Pharaoh to be an example of his judgment, but here is the point: the phrase is he showed great patience before he chose. Have you ever noticed that God hardened Pharaoh's heart three times, but only after Pharaoh had hardened his own heart seven times? Read the account carefully. Moses went to Pharaoh and said, "Let my people go," and Pharaoh refused – number one. He hardened his heart. After miracles of judgment on Egypt Moses goes again. Pharaoh says no again, but on the first, second, third, fourth, fifth, sixth, and seventh occasion, God did not do it. Pharaoh hardened his own heart, and it was then that God choose to harden his heart for him. That is the patience of the Lord. He does not arbitrarily choose one person for his judgment and one person for his mercy. He is patient with them to see which way they are choosing to go. Then he steps in and helps them to go the way they have chosen. So he was patient with Pharaoh. He didn't say, "I choose Pharaoh to be an example of my judgment" before Pharaoh was even born. He waited, and seven times Pharaoh hardened his own heart, and then God stepped in and said: Right, if that's the way you're choosing, I will now harden it further for you.

That is the choice of God in scripture. He waits patiently to see which way a person is choosing, and then he will help them to go down the road they have chosen to travel. That is the sovereignty of God in action. It is not arbitrary. It is not from our point of view a lottery whom God chooses. There is always a reason for it, and the reason is to be found in the person he chooses one way or the other. His choice of Pharaoh to be the ultimate object of his judgment was based on Pharaoh's own hardening of his own heart. There is a teaching of God's sovereignty that it is purely arbitrary as far as we are concerned – that he chooses one for heaven and another for hell utterly regardless of any reason. That would make salvation the biggest national lottery there has ever been, a matter of sheer luck as to whether God chooses you. But in fact, God chooses us with reasons, and he has the right to. If Pharaoh chooses to go that road, God has the perfect right to push him further down that road. That is his choice, and God is saying, "I'll confirm the choice, and I'll help you in it." That is a very important point.

Paul adds at this point that God's reason for choosing Jews was to reach the Gentiles. That comes out all through the Old Testament. "You are to be a light to the Gentiles." God did not choose the Jews to give them a special privilege because he has got no favourites. On judgment day we will all see that, but he did choose them. I think he chose them because they had nothing. They were a bunch of slaves – no nation of their own, no land of their own, no money of their own, nothing of their own. They were building pyramids for Pharaohs. They were slaves, and that is a typical choice of

God. He tells them in Deuteronomy, "I didn't choose you because you were a great people. I chose you because I chose you." He said, "I don't love you because you're special. I love you because I love you." The reason is to be found in God, not the Jews. Why did God choose the Jews? Well, look at God, don't look at the Jews.

They are a special people now. Through the ages they have had an astonishing effect on the rest of the world out of all proportion to their size. They are point one percent of the world's population, but they have supplied twenty-five percent of the world's scientists. That is an astonishing achievement. They are a little people with a huge impact on others. That is how God has made them. They have become shrewd and clever through the things that God has allowed to happen to them. They have supplied the majority of the world's entertainment in films. All five Hollywood studios were Jewish. In the fields of music, architecture, whatever you name, you will find Jews at the top of the profession out of all proportion to their numbers.

God meant them to be that special in leading the world to the truth of his religion. That was his calling. If they had been as good at sharing the gospel of Jesus with the world as they are at everything else, I don't think we would need any missionaries of our own. They would have had such an impact on the world! That is where they failed and failed badly, but God has not given up on them, as we shall see in chapter 11: they have broken the covenant with him, but he vowed that he would never break a covenant with them, and he has kept that covenant; it is his remnant, his right, his righteousness; it is our responsibility, and his reason for hardening some and softening others, we will find that reason in them. That is a summary of chapter nine.

Let us turn to the second great chapter, Chapter 10. In the present, they are stumbling. They are falling over Jesus instead of resting on him. If you have tried to evangelise Jews you will appreciate that they are the hardest people on earth to lead to Christ. The amazing thing is that for over 150 years Gentile missionaries have tried to lead Jews to the Lord and had little success. They have had some, but there are almost as many Jewish missionary societies as converted Jews! There has been a concerted effort, yet since 1948 the tide has totally turned, and it has not been Gentile missionaries who have done it, it has been Jews themselves. In 1948 you could count the number of believing Jews in Jesus in Jerusalem on two hands. Now in Israel alone there are 15,000 Israelis who believe in *Yeshua Ha Mashiach*. Worldwide there are now 45,000 Jews who share the Saviour with us. You must have heard of the *Jews for Jesus* movement. They are part of it. The most amazing thing is that since they got their land back thousands of them are turning to their Messiah, Jesus Christ. It all happened since 1948, and it is Jews leading Jews to faith in our Lord. That is one of the miracles that is happening in our lifetime. Before that, missionaries laboured for years, but now it is happening before our very eyes. There are over 70 indigenous Jewish fellowships worshipping Jesus in the land. Two of them alone are in the Israeli army, and it is happening!

There was a little girl in our church years ago at whose marriage I later officiated. She is now devoted to telling the world about the Jews and Arabs in the Middle East who are turning to Jesus. She has written a number of books. If you see a book by Julia Fisher it is all about how Jews and Arabs are often together in the Middle East. You will never hear of this in the papers. They ignore it, but up to a thousand Jews and Arabs are meeting secretly in the forests of Israel in the name of Jesus. I find that exciting. God is doing a new thing. He has brought them back to the land. He promised that when he did that he would bring them back to himself, and he is doing it on an unprecedented scale. We are the generation who are living to see his covenant with Israel fulfilled. That should give us a tremendous sense of privilege.

Let us move on to their stumbling in the present. Paul, though he is a Jewish Jew and is so loyal to his people, tells us the solid truth, which is that Gentiles are entering the kingdom in their millions and doing it so easily, and Jews are still the most difficult people on earth to get into the kingdom. It is a great anomaly in Paul's life, and there are two failures he underlines. First, there is their failure to achieve righteousness. He has already shown that in the Old Testament there are promises that there will be a remnant of Jews and a multitude of Gentiles coming to the Lord. He quotes Hosea and Isaiah to prove that God himself showed the Jews that he anticipated a great influx of Gentiles into the faith. That has happened, and the Jews still, most of them, are failing to achieve righteousness for one simple reason. They are trying to achieve a righteousness of their own instead of receiving the righteousness of God through the gospel. God does not want them to pretend their own righteousness to him. He wants to give them his, but there is something called human pride. It is very strong in the Gentile world too – that people would rather try to be good themselves than let God make them good, because when God shares his righteousness there is no room for boasting. Paul has already said that to the Romans. If you have to receive righteousness as a free gift, then how can you boast about achieving righteousness? Pride does not like to receive a gift. Pride says, "I'll work it up myself, thank you. I'll be good myself, thank you."

This is why they stumble over Christ. Christ came to bring them the righteousness of God and to give it to them as a free gift. They have turned it down because they want to achieve their own. This is basically why my hairdresser, as I have already mentioned, said, "I'm as good as anybody that goes to your church." He was thinking of self-righteousness. Do you know that that is the biggest barrier to the gospel? Not sins, not criminal acts, not cannibals or criminals – self-righteousness is the biggest barrier to the grace of God. People find it more difficult to repent of their good deeds than of bad deeds. It is awfully difficult to repent of your good deeds and not feel proud of being better than the man next door, and of having achieved things yourself. You will find that the Jews today (and I love them and they know that) are still, many of them, full of their own good works and what they do for each other and what they do for the world and what Israel does for Gentile nations who need them.

You would not believe what Israel as a nation does for non-Israelis. There is a poor African pastor whom I met at a Feast of Tabernacles, who had built up a large church in Africa. He was a good pastor and a good teacher, faithful to the Lord, but he was an ex-Muslim, and he was in a Muslim country. Just a year or so ago, when he came out of church on Christmas Eve, Muslims came up and threw acid in his face, which destroyed his face – the acid that fell onto the mudguards of his car which was eaten through with the acid. That man has to wear a complete mask with one hole for the one eye that he can still see through and a hole for his mouth and two holes for the nostrils so he can breathe. You talk to him and you just cannot see him at all. I have seen photographs of his face as it was left by the acid. It is a horrible sight. Think of his family – and yet you talk to him, he is one of the bravest men I know. The courage of the man! His ambition is to get back to his church and preach the gospel again. After some days of difficulty they managed to fly him to India. The hospital there could do nothing for him, so the Israeli hospital said, "We will care for him." They have rebuilt his faculties, and they are operating time and time again and gradually restoring him. They are doing it out of the goodness of their heart.

Do you know that Israeli hospitals are looking after Syrians who have been wounded in their own country? I have never known a nation do so much even for people who were their enemies, but the trouble is it makes them proud. They are proud of their achievements. They are proud of having built a prospering country. They are one of the few countries in the world with a growing economy, clear economy, and they are proud of it. They have achieved so much. They have turned a barren, desolate, empty land that could not support more than a few Bedouins, and it now supports a population of seven million including many Arabs. You never hear all this, do you?

There is an anti-Semitic prejudice in the mass media, which becomes very more obvious as the days go by. But they are still stumbling over Jesus, who came to be their Saviour, their Messiah, came to bring the righteousness of God to them. He came to do everything they really needed because all their achievements are in other fields, in technology particularly. They have invented a machine the size of my briefcase for dialysis of kidneys. You only need to plug it in to an ordinary cold tap of water to make it work. Whereas many people with kidney trouble have to go for hours into a hospital and be hooked up and stay there twice a week to get the blood clean, this invention of Israel you can carry with you to a hotel and plug it into the cold water tap and dialyse your own kidneys, clean your blood.

Their technical inventions are outstanding, and the world is benefitting from all this, but as far as telling the world what they were meant to be – a light to the Gentiles that would shine up for God – they have been and still are as a nation a complete failure. They stumble over the rock on which they could have stood. It is as if Jesus is in the middle of the road in front of them, and they fall over him. They have missed him. That is their tragedy, and it was because they established their own righteousness through works of the law. "They're zealous for God," says Paul, "yet without knowledge." There is an ignorance that prevents them from seeing Jesus as he really is. So there is the rock in front of them, and here are Gentiles who have had no preparation. There are people like you and me who were not born into their privileges, and we are finding our way and so easily! This is the irony of history – that there are millions and millions of Gentiles walking into the kingdom so easily while the Jews are stumbling over the very person who could have helped them in.

Their next failure which Paul mentions is the failure to receive revelation. They have heard but not heeded. They have understood but not undertaken, and so I want to look now at the logic of Paul. It is very straightforward logic. He says: "Salvation is as near to human beings as your mouth and your heart." You don't have to climb up to heaven to find Christ. You don't have to dig down into the world of the departed to find Christ. Christ is so near to you, as near as your own breathing. Simply confessing him with your mouth and believing in your heart – it is as near as that to every Jew. All they need do is confess him.

I remember preaching in Ely, a town near Cambridge in England, and in the congregation was a young Jewish lady. I would put her about twenty-five perhaps – a Jewess in a church for the very first time. Somebody persuaded her to come and hear me. She came straight up after the service and said, "Are you trying to tell me that Jesus of Nazareth is still alive?" Interesting she called him Jesus of Nazareth, which was his title in their eyes.

I replied, "Well actually, yes. That's why I'm here."

She said, "But if Jesus is still alive, he must be *our* Messiah" – not the Christ, our Messiah.

"That's true."

"How could I find out if he's alive?"

I said, "Come with me." I took her to the vestry at the back of the church, sat her down in a comfortable chair, and said, "I'm going to leave you for fifteen minutes on your own, and I want you to talk to Jesus – to talk aloud to Jesus. If he is alive, he will talk back. That is a simple thing for you to do. Tell him about yourself. Tell him what you think of him; tell him everything that is in your heart. Just talk to him." Then I went away and left her.

I came back after fifteen minutes; I opened the door, and she sprang out of the chair and said, "He's alive! He's alive!" You know, within five minutes she was teaching me the Bible. Then she said, "Then this is true, and this must be true." She had got it all in her. It was in her blood. She knew all the prophecies, and now she knew that Jesus of Nazareth was alive. That is all the Jew needs to know.

That is what happened to Saul of Tarsus on the Damascus Road.

"Who are you, Lord?"

"I'm Jesus, whom you're persecuting."

That was the moment when Paul got his doctrine of the body of Christ being the church. He realised immediately that what you do to Christians you are doing to Christ. Persuade a Jew that Jesus is alive. That is all they need. They will turn, and when Jesus gets back and appears to the Jewish nation, guess what will happen? It is as simple as that.

We have been rushing ahead to chapter 11. Now let us get back to chapter 10.

They have heard. How shall anybody call on the name of the Lord if they have not heard about him? How will they hear about him unless somebody preaches to them? How will someone preach to them unless they have been sent by God? It is very logical. They have to hear about Christ and they will not hear unless someone goes to preach to them. Someone won't go to preach to them unless God sends them. You can see God's plan in all this. Then Paul says they do know. They have heard. He quotes Psalm nineteen, which is about the sun that rises in the morning and floods the whole world with light, and everybody knows about the sun. He simply says: "But they also know about the Son of God." It is a fact – you try to talk to them – that every Jew has heard about Jesus. They know; they have heard. That is not the problem. The problem is that they have not heeded it.

Isaiah said of Israel, "They have ears but they don't take it in. They have hearts but they don't understand." Poor Isaiah was called of God to be a failure as a preacher. It is an amazing call of God, and when people read about the call of Isaiah, they always stop at the vital verse and don't go on. They stop at the verse where Isaiah says, "Here am I! Send me." He's butting in on a conversation in heaven where God the Father to the Son and the Spirit is saying: "Whom shall we send, and who will go for us?" Isaiah said, "Here am I!" It was after God had burned his lips with a live coal from the altar. Isaiah was the prophet with the scarred lips forever afterwards. People must have asked him, "How did you get a mouth like that?" He said, "I was a man of unclean lips, and God cleansed my lips with a fiery coal from the altar." Then God said, "Go! You said, 'Here am I! Send me,' then go and tell this people you hear but you won't take it in: you will get the message and reject it."

Isaiah was told that for the rest of his life he would be a failure as a preacher, and the more he preached the less they would respond. He finished up, poor soul, in a terrible death. He was tied and bound and pushed into a hollow tree trunk, and then they sawed the tree trunk in two and sawed him in two. He is referred to in Hebrews 11: "Some were sawn asunder." It is a horrible way to die. He had been a failure as a preacher his whole life. The more he preached, the harder the audience became and the more difficult it became to get it through.

Yet Isaiah never knew that his book of prophecies would become the greatest prophecy of the Old Testament. I hope you have read it and studied it. If not, get my book on Isaiah, but it is the most thrilling prophecy that is more quoted than any other in the New Testament. Isaiah never lived to see that. He was a failure as a preacher, and the words he used about the Jews – that they would hear it but never understand it – was quoted by Jesus about his parables when he was asked, "Why do you speak in parables?" He quoted Isaiah: "It is so that they will hear but not understand." Paul himself quoted it when he came to preach to the Jews in Rome when he was taken there as a prisoner. He was free to speak to the Jews there, and he did so. When they rejected his message, he said, "Well did Isaiah speak of you." It is a sad story.

It is characteristic of the Jew today that his heart is hard against the gospel of Christ. It is not that they haven't heard and it is not even that they haven't understood. One of the saddest verses in chapter 10 is towards the end, where God says, "I've held out my hands to you all day long, and I've had no response." That is the God who is sovereign. He holds out his hands to plead with people. You can preach the sovereignty of God in such a hard way that you forget that he is the God who is patient and the God who pleads with people to respond. He doesn't make people respond. That is not how he uses his sovereignty. He holds out his hands: Please, I want to help you. I want to share my righteousness. I want to make you the people you long to be in your best moments. There is a pleading God there. They have heard, and they would not accept. They are stubborn, and therefore they are stumbling.

If that were the end of the story of the Jews it would be

a really sad thing, but it is not. We turn to chapter 11 which says that they will be saved in the future. That is a promise and a mystery, a secret that Paul was allowed to reveal. It is the last thing the world would think. The world says the Jews deserve all they get. Do you know that for centuries the church accused the Jews of killing Jesus? In fact it was Gentiles who did the actual killing. It was my sin that put Jesus on the cross, so who am I to blame the Jews for killing Jesus? The church never thought like that, and the history of the church's anti-Semitism over two thousand years is a horrible history. There is a museum in Tel Aviv which everybody ought to go and see, but hardly anybody does because it is not in Jerusalem. Most Christians want to see Jerusalem, but they don't go to Tel Aviv. There is a museum telling the story of the Jews for the last two thousand years of which most Christians are totally ignorant. When you go into the museum there are projectors in the ceiling in the entrance hall that project Jewish faces onto the floor and you cannot get into the museum without walking on those Jewish faces. It is to tell you how they have felt for two thousand years. Most of the troubles they have experienced in their scattered Diaspora came from the church.

Consider the record of the first preaching against the Jews, when the church got power under Constantine. Then the church closed synagogues. They made Jews wear yellow stars. They did all sorts of things – shut them up in ghettos. Christians did this! Martin Luther was one of the worst. At first he thought that if he preached the simple gospel to the Jews they would respond, but he found, as everybody else does, that they are stubborn, that they hear but don't take it in, and so he turned right against them. Martin Luther preached a sermon that was an appeal to Germany to get rid of the Jews. He said, "Burn the synagogues down. Destroy their books. Banish the rabbis. Take their passports from them." He died just a few days later and that was the final sermon he ever preached. To this day the Lutheran Church of Germany is largely anti-Semitic and believes in replacement theology – that the church has taken their place and that God has rejected his ancient people.

Paul begins chapter 11 with a question again. "I ask, has God rejected the Jews?" You know the answer: "Never!" Later in the chapter he says, "Have the Jews fallen beyond hope? Will they never recover? Never!" Here is a chapter that is not the favourite chapter to be preached in church unfortunately, but it is a chapter that says God has not rejected them. God has not gone back on them. Then he says, "Let's look at their past." First, God always kept a remnant. He quotes the prophet Elijah. When Elijah was challenged by the prophets of Baal, he won the challenge and then fled for his life from Jezebel, who was angry. One angry woman turned that brave prophet into a coward, and he ran away. He had a conversation with God, and he said, "God, you wanted a people on earth. I'm the only one left – even I." God told Elijah that his mathematics were a bit wrong and he still had got a few thousand faithful. He still had a remnant. Paul quotes that in chapter 11 and adds "and to this day". God kept a remnant of faithful Jews, and they are still his people. He has not broken any promise to them or broken any covenant with them. By grace he has kept them – not because grace is an irresistible force, but they have been able to receive grace by faith. God then keeps them to himself. It is not of works, but by their faith he has kept them.

What has happened then to the rest of the Jews? If the remnant has been kept, the rest have been hardened. God's hardening activity has come in. They have hardened their hearts against God, so God has said, "If that's the way you want to go, I'll help you." God has hardened the Jews. This happens whenever the word of God is preached. Some are softened and some are hardened. It could even happen when I try to share with you the truth of Romans. You will either be softened or hardened, and it will depend on the attitude you come with. I hope that you have a softening heart ready to receive truth. You will get it. You will be blessed, but if anyone comes with a heart that is suspicious, beginning to harden against the truth, then God will harden it for you. He will help you down the road that you have chosen. God hardens people as well as softens them, and that depends on them.

That is what has happened in the past. A remnant has been held and the rest have been hardened, so what is happening in the present? Well, funnily enough, because the Jews rejected the gospel it came to Gentiles. We should be actually very thankful to the Jews for rejecting it because we got it. Everywhere Paul went and preached first to the Jews, when they rejected it, he said, "I turn to the Gentiles. They'll receive it" – and they did. We are the result. The gospel came west into Europe because of Paul. Paul travelled with the gospel because the Jewish nation rejected it. That is a reason to be profoundly grateful to the Jews, but Paul adds, "We should use this to make them jealous." Unfortunately the NIV has rendered this: to make them envious. No, the Jews rejected and it came to us Gentiles so that we could make them jealous. I must explain as clearly as I can the difference between being envious and being jealous. If I meet somebody whose wife I find attractive, I might be envious. (This has not happened to me yet!) But if someone ran away with my wife, I would be jealous. In both cases I would be angry, but in one case the anger would be envious, and in the other case it would be jealous. In other words, to make a Jew jealous is not saying, "We've got something you haven't," but, "We found something you have." You can make a Jew jealous. "We have your scriptures; we have found the Jewish

Messiah." That makes them jealous, not saying, "We've found the Lord and you haven't." That would be trying to make them envious. God has brought the gospel to us after the Jews rejected it to make them jealous, to make them say, "That's ours! It was ours before theirs!" When that Jewess in Ely said to me, "If Jesus is alive, he must be our Messiah," then jealousy was beginning to rise in her heart. Do you understand? That is the missionary method with Jews. That was Paul's method. Arouse their jealousy; tell them that you have discovered what belongs to them, what is their right, what is their past, what is their heritage, not something we have discovered that is our heritage, but what was theirs we have discovered for ourselves.

So the good thing in the present is making Jews jealous, but the bad thing is that it has made Gentiles arrogant. Make the Jews jealous, yes, but don't get proud of the fact that you accepted what they rejected. That is the danger for the Gentile church. The church has fallen into that – hook, line, and sinker – and has become proud of accepting what Jews rejected. This leads to an attitude of contempt for the Jewish people if we are not careful, and "replacement theology", as we call it – that claim that the church has replaced Israel, that we are the new Israel of God, that we are now the chosen people. That is arrogance, and now Paul has reached the point of the whole letter. Three times in chapter 11 he accuses the Gentile believers of Rome of arrogance, of boasting. You can't have arrogance without contempt. You can't be proud of yourself without looking down on someone else. The two are inevitable, two sides of the same coin. If you are proud as a Gentile because you accepted what they rejected, you will have contempt for them.

That is when Paul makes some very strong statements. First of all he says an amazing thing: "If their rejection of Christ brought the gospel to the world, what will their acceptance be but life from the dead?" It is a logical argument. He is saying: if their rejection meant so much to the rest of the world, how much more will their acceptance mean? He doesn't say it as a hypothetical "if". He says it will happen. He doesn't say, "If the Jews came to Christ, what a blessing that would be." He is saying *when* they come to Christ. He is absolutely sure they are going to. He said if their rejection brought such blessing to the Gentiles, what will their acceptance be but life from the dead?

Can you imagine a world in which you open your front door and two well-dressed young men from Israel have come to tell you about Jesus? Not Jehovah's Witnesses. Actually God had said to them through Isaiah: "'You will be my witnesses,' says Jehovah." He has called them to be Jehovah's witnesses, but then they have not done it. There will come a day when two young men from Israel will knock at your door and say, "We've come to tell you the good news!" They will be sending young men from Israel all over the world to tell the world. At last they will fulfil their calling. Paul has no doubt about it. There's no "if" about it – what will happen when they accept?

The most gifted people on earth; the most amazing people on earth who have done so much for the world already; you have benefitted today from the Jewish people. Have you used a telephone today? A Jew invented it. Do you travel by plane? A Jew invented the aeroplane. Did you have a tomato for breakfast? It was a Jew who discovered the tomato. Have you ever had an injection of cocaine to have a tooth filled to stop you having pain? It was a Jew who invented that. I could just go through your daily life and show you how much you have already benefitted from the Jewish people, but you did not get your faith from them. That is the tragedy. You got it from another Gentile, almost certainly. But if we got all that through their rejection, what will happen when they accept their own Messiah and Lord? The mind boggles.

So we make Jews jealous if possible, without making ourselves arrogant. That is a very important point. Paul goes on to say yes, there has been some replacement. Some of the Jewish branches of the olive tree were cut out, and you Gentiles have been grafted in, in their place. You notice that it is *some* Jews were cut out. You were grafted in the place of some Jews among the others. It is a very Jewish tree, and we Gentiles have been grafted into the Jewish tree. Paul says you don't support the tree – the tree supports you. Our faith has Jewish roots. If your faith is rooted in this Bible, your faith is rooted in Jewish roots. It is the roots that support you. You don't support them. It is a very strong argument.

Now Paul dares to say something that may come as a shock. He said, "If God cut some of the Jews out when they lost their faith in him, he will also cut you out if you lose your faith in him." Now take that very seriously. To cut their arrogance out, he said, "Serve the Lord with fear" – because he is the same God. The God of Israel cut some Jews out, and he will also cut Christians out if they do not maintain their faith, if they do not continue in God's kindness; you too will be cut off. That is why I don't believe "once saved, always saved". That is why I said about the end of Romans 8, which promises that nothing can separate us, that you can separate yourself. If you don't go on believing in Jesus till the end, you too will be cut off. It could not be said in a plainer way. Don't get arrogant because some Jews were cut out. You too will be cut out if you do what they did – and they lost their trust in God.

He is referring, of course, to the fact that a huge number, 600,000, came out of Egypt, and only two of them got into the promised land. What happened to the rest? They were cut out. They died in the wilderness. They never made it, and that is used in the New Testament as a warning to Christian believers. It is not the faith you start with that saves you. It is the faith you finish with that saves you. "He that endures to the end will be saved." Every time the word, "believe" comes in John's Gospel, it is in a special Greek tense called the present continuous tense, which means to *go on* doing something; not to do it once, but to do it for the rest of your life. "For God so loved the world, that he gave his only-begotten Son, that whoever *goes on believing in him* will never perish but *go on having* eternal life." Jesus said, "Abide in me; stay in me. If you don't stay in me, you will become fruitless; you will wither, and the gardener will prune those dead branches out and throw them into the fire." As that is what Jesus said, I cannot believe the cliché "once saved, always saved." There are eighty passages of scripture I could quote to you that say don't lose what you've got in Christ. Every writer of the New Testament has given us a warning that you could lose your salvation.

The proof is the Jews who died in the wilderness. They did not make it because they did not trust God and obey him. They had sent spies into the promised land from Kadesh-barnea and the twelve spies came back. Ten of them said, "You won't get in there. The cities have walls as high as heaven and the people are much bigger than we are. They are giants in the land." Ten of the spies said, "There is no point in us going any further." Two of the spies, Joshua and one other, said, "We go in on God's shoulders, and on God's shoulders we are taller than the giants. We look over the walls, and God will pull them down for us." They were the only two who got in. The rest of them believed the ten spies who said, "We won't make it." They fell in the wilderness. It can happen to Christians too, simply because God is the same God and deals with people in the same way. So we need to learn from the Old Testament and be grateful to God.

We come to this amazing verse: "God has grafted you

wild olives into the olive tree of Israel." Now that is quite an amazing thing for a gardener to do. When you graft in a shoot from the same roots, that stands a much better chance of growing back in. He says God can graft Jews back in to their own tree. "Furthermore," he says – and here is the mystery – "God will graft the whole nation back in." How will he do that? By removing the hardening of their hearts, by softening their hearts again, and we are told one day it will be Israel as a whole – not necessarily every Jew then living, certainly not every Jew who has ever lived but the nation as a whole. That is what "all Israel" means. It is that phrase from the Old Testament, "All Israel gathered to King David." It does not mean that every man, woman and child was there. It means that representatives of the twelve tribes came to meet David. One day that will happen – they will come to the Son of David and will be joined to the church as one olive tree, one new man in Christ Jesus. That is the meaning of the word "saved" there. It does not promise they will be saved from the Arabs or from anyone else, it will be saved from their sins, as it was for us, and in the same way: by trusting in Jesus.

So one day God will show mercy to them by softening their hearts. I believe he will do it when he sends Jesus, who is coming back not to London, not to Washington, not to Beijing but back to Jerusalem to his own people. They will see him again. It says, "They will weep as for an only son," when they realise what they have been doing for two thousand years, stumbling over the rock that was meant to be the rock on which they stood. They will repent as a nation. That is promised in scripture, in Romans 11. I believe it, and what will happen then? I just can't imagine, but it will be good.

Now Paul finishes by saying, "Do you see then that the salvation of the Jew and of the Gentile are interlinked?"

The rejection of the Jew brought God's mercy to the Gentile. God's mercy coming to the Gentiles will make the Jews jealous, and it will go back to them. Concerning our salvation, at one point God actually says that is for the sake of the Jews. He is saving us Gentiles so that he can save them. Our futures are interlinked. We are all heading for a city with a Jewish name and with twenty-four Jewish names inscribed on the foundations in the walls and the gates – the New Jerusalem is where we are heading. We are all going to be one people in a very Jewish city, the New Jerusalem, which God is already building up there and will come down to the new earth.

The thought of all this! How God has interwoven the story of the Jews and the story of the Gentiles together, and Jesus said, "I have other sheep that don't belong to this fold [meaning Israel], them also I must bring" – and there will be one fold and one shepherd. Our future is with the Jews. Our destiny is theirs. We are all interlocked, and this so overwhelms Paul to see how God is working all this out in history – it so overwhelms him that he has to burst out in praise. He stops teaching and he starts praising God for his inscrutable wisdom, for his independent action, and for his indispensable presence. In famous words, "For from him and through him and to him are all things, to him be the glory for ever. Amen."

6. RELATIONSHIPS

ROMANS 12:1–13:14

A WITH GOD (12:1-8)
  1. DO – SACRIFICE (1-2)
      a. Dedicated bodies
            i. Physical waiver
            ii. Spiritual worship
      b. Decontaminated minds
            i. Mental discipline
            ii. Moral direction
  2. DON'T – SNOBBERY (3-8)
      a. Measured faith
            i. Selfish arrogance
            ii. Sober assessment
      b. Multiple functions
            i. Example
            ii. Exercise

B WITH PEOPLE (12:9-21)
  1. INSIDERS – HARMONY (9-16)
      a. DO – genuine caring
            i. For one another
            ii. For one's self
      b. DON'T – false conceit
            i. Association
            ii. Arrogance
  2. OUTSIDERS – HOSTILITY (17-21)
      a. DON'T – retaliation
            i. Human revenge
            ii. Divine vengeance
      b. DO – reconciliation
            i. Words – blessings for curses
            ii. Deeds – good for evil

C WITH GOVERNMENT (13:1-14)
   1. DO – AUTHORITY (1-7)
      a. Civic dignity
          i. Establishment (provision, protection)
          ii. Punishment (commendation, condemnation)
      b. Citizen duty
          i. Submit (cowardice, conscience)
          ii. Support (revenue, respect)

   2. DON'T – MORALITY (8-14)
      a. Fulfilling the law
          i. Monetary debts
          ii. Moral debt
      b. Understanding the time
          i. Wake up! (night and day)
          ii. Get dressed (darkness and light)

PLEASE READ ROMANS 12:1–13:14

In Romans 12–13, Paul deals with relationships, which are all important in life. The first relationship we need to get right is our relationship with God. We are justified. We are right with God, but there is an ongoing relationship with him that needs to be kept fresh and real. This whole section is full of dos and don'ts. Almost every section tells us what to do and what not to do. The Jews had 613 dos and don'ts in the law of Moses, but do you know how many we have in the new covenant? Over 1100! There are dos and don'ts for the Christian. The difference is that the Christian believer, full of the Holy Spirit, wants to do the "dos" and does not want to do the "don'ts". In this part of Paul's letter there are practical dos and don'ts.

Let us look first then at the dos and don'ts for our relationships with God. The first "do" is to sacrifice to God. The whole notion of sacrifice to us is quite strange. We don't go to church on a Sunday morning carrying a lamb or a pigeon or some little creature that our pastor is going to cut the throat of in the front of the church. Worship would be a bit of a bloodbath. We are not into that because God has made it obsolete. That sacrifice has ended. God is asking now for a living sacrifice. All the Old Testament ones were dead. They were killed and then they were offered. In the new covenant God requires living sacrifices, so Paul pleads: "I urge you by the mercies of God...."

That takes us back to the end of Chapter 11 on the mercy of God, a wonderful theme, and in that passage, God said he chained up the Gentiles in disobedience and chained up the Jews in disobedience, in order that he might have mercy on all of them. There was a well-known public character having his portrait painted to hang in a public place, and he said to the artist, "I hope this portrait will do me justice." The artist replied, "It's not justice you need, it's mercy." Now you know what mercy is. Justice is what we deserve, but mercy is what we don't deserve. That is how God wants the relationship between him and us to be. This is about the mercies of God, the undeserved grace of God, the thing we never deserved – it is by this that Paul will appeal.

Now I will tell you a little secret. My wife can't start the day without a daily fix, which is a cup of tea. She has to have that cup of tea in the morning, and so, since we married, I have got into the habit as well. If I wake up in the morning and I feel like a Christian first thing, I make the tea. If I don't feel like a Christian when I wake up, she has to go and make it. That is an arrangement we have. I won't tell you what the ratio is between my making it and her making it. If I make it, I go downstairs, out of the front door, and pick up two bottles of milk because we get our milk delivered. The bottles are cold and sometimes frozen, and if the morning is cold too it is quite miserable to go out and pick up those cold things. I come in hugging them, and I never forget one text in the book of Lamentations as I come in: "Your mercies are fresh every morning." As I carry them back in, I thank God for his mercies. Yes, I am eighty-four, but I am still able to work for the Lord. That is a mercy! I don't deserve it. We have moved to a little retirement flat and we have that place we can call our own. That is a mercy! I didn't deserve that. I have got health, work to do and a place to live. Every one of those things is undeserved, and I count the mercies, which are fresh every morning. The first time you disobeyed God you locked yourself into a prison – that God might have mercy on you and give you something you never deserved or could deserve. By the mercies of God, then, give him a living sacrifice. It is a physical one, as all the other Old Testament sacrifices were physical. This time it is your body, a living sacrifice, which you present to him. The word "present" there is in the Greek text and means to do it *once for all*. Not to do it every day, but once for all to say, "Lord, here's my body for you to use." Did you notice in Chapter 6, for example: "Present your bodies as instruments of righteousness." What you do with your body is very important. It is why a former Archbishop of Canterbury, William Temple, said that Christianity is the most materialistic religion in the whole world. It is to do with bodies, physical things. "Present your bodies, then, once for all." Waive your right to your own body just once, and do it permanently. That is the living sacrifice that God wants now. Then, astonishingly, that is your spiritual worship.

There was a young student in Cambridge who went to a missionary meeting. The time came when they passed the plate round for the collection, he put his hand in his pocket and realised he had left his wallet at home. He didn't know what to do as the plate drew nearer. As it came to his row in the meeting he pulled out his pen and notebook, and he wrote something on a piece of paper, tore it out and put it in the collection. It was not an IOU. He simply wrote this word on the paper: Myself. He finished up as one of the best-known missionaries in India. It was the biggest thing put on the collection plate, and he did it. Here is my body. Send it where you wish. It is a big sacrifice to waive any right to your own body.

He wants your minds too. The moral of the next verse is this: don't be a chameleon, be a caterpillar. That is the meaning of the next verse. Do you know what a chameleon is? It is an animal that if you put it on any colour it changes colour according to its background. Don't take the colour of your thinking from people around you, or as J.B. Phillips translated it, "Don't let the world around you squeeze you into its own mould." If we take all our thoughts from television, the internet and the other mass media, that will colour your thinking. If you spend more time watching television than reading your Bible, which is going to colour your thinking?

That is why you need to spend time with the Word of God until you think like God thinks, until you feel like God feels, until your mind has been transformed from within. That is why he wants you to be a caterpillar. Caterpillars are rather ugly things when they start. Then they become a chrysalis and that too is rather ugly – a chrysalis is attached to a branch of a flower. It is being changed from the inside until suddenly one day it bursts and out comes a beautiful butterfly. All those colours were formed inside, out of sight until they came out. So don't be a chameleon, be a caterpillar; let the colours of your thinking come from the inside, not the outside – not from the people in the world, but from the transformation within of your thinking.

These are the two things that God is waiting for from us: a dedicated body and a decontaminated mind – that is no longer contaminated by the world around. When he has got that, then he is prepared to guide you into his will for you. After all, why should he show you what his will is for you before he has your body and mind? It would be pretty useless to guide you before he has those two things, but when he has got them you will then test and approve his will for you. That is the path to guidance as far as I understand it. Make the sacrifice of your body first, colour your mind from within until your mind is his mind. Then you will know what he wants you to do, because then he can use you. You will find that that will of his for you is perfect and pleasing. It becomes just what you were made for, and to get to the end of life and feel that you have known and done his will must be the most satisfying life. To get to the end of life and wonder if you did must be terrible. To have no regrets when you reach the end of the road – that will be because you made the sacrifice and he told you what to do with what you gave him.

We have covered the first two verses of Chapter 12 and now we move on. There is a don't in this as well: don't let what he gives you turn you into a religious snob. We have always got to watch that. When we know his will and do it, don't be proud about it. Don't get big-headed about it. Stay humble. Measure your faith, and of course our faith, by which we live and work, is given to us by God. He knows how much faith we need and how much we need to do his will. So don't get big ideas. The measure of your faith is a sure measurement of where you are in God's will. Think soberly about how much faith is given you and how you are using it. That is one factor; that is considering yourself.

In avoiding spiritual snobbery, the second part is to realise that yours is only one gift among many and that all the gifts need each other. If God gives you a gift of healing for other people, it is not to make you a famous healer. It is to fit you in with the other gifts in the body, so that together as a multiple function the body operates. It does not matter if you are a visible part of the body or an invisible part of the body, you are just as important. If God has given you a gift, don't get excited about it, use it! If your gift is teaching, then teach. If your gift is healing, then heal. He lists a lot of gifts and is saying: use those gifts; don't treasure them; don't shut them up and put them away, but use them in the multiple-function body of Christ which needs every gift working together with the others. All that will keep you in your place. Your gift is not so that you can be admired. Your gift is given for the body, so use it with the others.

Seven gifts are listed here. You can read them through and think about them. *Prophecy* (that's not preaching) is a gift that anybody in the congregation can exercise. Prophecy is to give a word from the Lord straight away, without premeditation, a word that the Lord wants to pass on through someone's mouth – whether about the past, the present, or the future – to the people of God. Use it if you have that gift. Not all have it.

Service – the word literally is "deacon". "In your diaconate," says Paul. If your calling is as a deacon to care for the practical needs of the saints, then you get on with that. Some people who are better with their hands than their heads, who can do something very practical – get on with it, use it. It is a gift.

Teaching – the applying of truth to the hearts of men – is that the gift God gave you? Then use it.

All these are gifts that have to be stirred up. Once you have got a gift you need to develop it. With teaching or with deacons, or whatever the gift may be, you need to use it and develop it.

Exhorting – this means encouraging people. God needs in every church some people with the gift of encouraging others. Not everybody has this gift. Some people just discourage others! Exhortation means appealing to their will rather than their mind – to get on with the job.

Contributing – you know what that means. "He that contributes..." in other words, if you're in a position to give, then do it with liberality. Let it flow; don't be niggardly and mean.

He who is called to lead – How important it is that someone who is prominent in the church should be zealous, not slack and lazy and "any old thing will do." If the leaders of a church are slack and lazy, can you blame a church for not getting anywhere? If the leaders are zealous, enthusiastic and giving themselves sacrificially, you will have a church that will follow.

Finally, if your job is doing acts of *mercy* – maybe visiting the sick or the sad – do it with cheerfulness. You go into someone's home and they are very ill in bed, tired and in pain, and you say, "Dear me, you are looking bad." Well, I'm sure they appreciate the sympathy, but it is not an act of mercy! Do it with cheerfulness. Let that overflow. The Lord loves cheerfulness; he loves a cheerful giver – those who can serve and do things for others cheerfully. The opposite is *reluctantly*....

"Will you please go and visit so and so sometime this week?"

"Well, let's see my diary. I might manage to fit it in. Yes, maybe Thursday night."

What a difference when someone says, "Yes, I'd love to." If you do acts of mercy, do it cheerfully. Isn't this practical? Dear me, isn't it far from what we are?

Faith – if you assess yourself according to the measure of faith, you will be able to work in unity and as part of the body. If you are useful in Christian works and do it heartily and with your whole soul, the church will be built up.

A German Christian preacher came to speak to Christian young people in England. He had been a leader in the Hitler Youth but he was converted as a prisoner of war in England during the war, by the Christians who showed him kindness here. He was asked, "What is your impression of Christian young people in Britain?"

He said this, "I'm concerned with the casual quality of their faith. They do not give Christ anything like the devotion we gave to Hitler."

I use that not to get at young people but to apply it to all of us. Do we give the same devotion to Christ that others give to human causes, human leaders, and human societies? "Whatsoever you find to do, do it with thy might." Thomas Carlyle gave that as a motto to a young man who wanted some good advice, and of course he took it from the Bible.

Turning to our attitude to others, each of the verses now is self-explanatory. Some of the teaching is from the book of Proverbs, one of the wisdom books of the Old Testament. Some is taken from the Sermon on the Mount, which is the heart of the wisdom of the New Testament. It is a portrait of Christian love and the equivalent in the Epistle to the Romans of 1 Corinthians 13. In the first four chapters of Romans you deal with faith, and in the next eight chapters you deal with hope, but for the last four chapters you deal with love.

Love is very offensive if it is pretended (v. 9). Let love be genuine. True love is compatible with hatred. If you really love, then you hate what is evil, you abhor it and you are glued to what is good—that is a literal translation. The next verse tells us that the world struggles to get honour for itself. Christians want to give honour to each other. What an extraordinary picture of a human society that is – and only the church, I think, could possibly achieve it, and often it fails to do so. The word used here for brotherly affection is family love. We are not a religious club, we are not a society, we are not an organisation—we are a family. Therefore, brotherly affection is the right thing.

Verse 11 talks of our *enthusiasm*, that vital glow. People who are in Christ should be at "boiling point" (in Revelation 3:14ff we learn what Jesus has to say about lukewarm people). Think of the gospel we have to preach, Christ whom we have as Saviour, the heaven we are going to – and to be lukewarm is unforgiveable. Piping hot! That is what it says here. "Be aglow with the Spirit, vital, warm, enthusiastic, full of the zeal of the Lord." We are to be optimistic, rejoicing in hope. There are no hopeless situations. We are to be full of hope. Even in present trouble, we are to be patient, and the only way to do this is to be constant in prayer.

Then, in practice, we are to have an open hand and an

open home. It is characteristic of a true Christian that they have an open hand to their fellow saints and an open home. *Hospitality* is enjoined upon us by almost every New Testament writer. Your home is not your own. You may have the mortgage or the deeds, but it is not yours when you are a Christian, it is Christ's house and he wants the front door and the back door wide open to any who come.

In v. 15, "Rejoice with those who rejoice, weep with those who weep." Which is the hardest to do? I'll tell you what I think: to rejoice with those who rejoice. It is human to be sympathetic. When someone is really going through deep sorrow, it is comparatively easy to feel the sorrow with them if you have any sensitivity at all. But when somebody has been successful or honoured, is it so easy to rejoice with them? A Christian shares his fellow believers' lives, and if they are happy, he congratulates them without any envy. If they are sad, he gives them condolence without any reserve. We are to live in harmony and peace with other people, with two conditions: firstly, if it be possible; secondly, insofar as in us lies – on our side.

So, having sorted out our continuing relationship with God, Paul moved on in chapter 12 to the relationships with people, especially first with God's people, the insiders, and then with the outsiders. Relationships with both those groups are important to the believer. If your relationship with God is right, then there are other relationships that don't happen automatically. You need to go on to get these right as well. First, with the insiders, the relationship is intended to be one of harmony so that all those inside the body of Christ are working harmoniously together. The word peace, or *shalom*, means harmony – harmony with God, harmony with yourself, harmony with other people, and harmony with nature; but here he is writing about the harmony that should exist in the body of Christ. Without harmony in the body of Christ the church cannot operate.

I went to one church, and I thought, "What's wrong with this church? I just can't get anywhere. There's no response." I won't tell you where it was in England, but it was really quite depressing. I knew there was something seriously wrong, and afterwards I was told that the church was divided totally into two halves. They even came into the church for worship through separate entrances and then sat on two sides of the church. I could hardly believe that such a state could exist, but each half was led by one of the leaders and the two leaders were not on speaking terms. There were a lot of people in that church. Little wonder that they were hopeless as a body. Well, that was an exaggerated case, but it can be found in a lesser degree in other churches.

So harmony is the objective of your relationship with everybody in your local church. A church is a mixed variety of people, and you relate to them all. A local church where there are rich and poor, cultured and uneducated, whether black or white people (God is colour-blind), and we need to be in churches that are as mixed as possible. God's people are mixed. For the purposes of evangelism and influence we may need to be in a more homogenous group that have more in common and share careers and interests. That is good, but we need to belong to a church which is a complete mixture of people – where we will have to associate with all possible different kinds of people.

The most flourishing churches in Britain at the moment are the so-called "black churches". They are filled with immigrants who have that in common, from the West Indies and from Nigeria particularly. They are very much made up of people who are already sharing an identity. There are some of them who have a little smattering of white folk among them, but they have an overwhelming majority of people who have got colour in common. I was thrilled when the first

Messianic Jewish assembly started in London some years ago. They rang me up and said, "David, would you consider becoming an elder of this fellowship?" I said, "I'm very touched that you asked, because I'm a Gentile; I'm a goy." They said, "But we don't want to be an exclusive Messianic fellowship." I said, "Logistically it's impossible for me to fulfil the duties of an elder to you. I live fifty miles away." I was touched that they wanted a goy in their eldership from the beginning, that they didn't want to be an exclusive Jewish fellowship, because again, while they were worshipping the same Lord they would be an identified group. The glory of the church is that it is for anybody and everybody. Happy are you if you are in a church where there is a great variety of people with whom you can learn that harmony.

At this point, Paul has a machine gun, and he fires bullet after bullet at the people inside the church. Just reading them is enough to knock you down. "Hate what is evil. Cling to what's good. Be devoted to one another. Honour one another above yourself. Never be lacking in zeal. Keep your spiritual fervour. Serve the Lord. Be joyful in hope; patient in affliction; faithful in prayer. Share with God's people who are in need. Practise hospitality. Rejoice with those who rejoice; mourn with those who mourn. Live in harmony with one another." Each of those would make a good sermon! Many of those "bullets" are concerned with others, but quite a few of them are concerned with yourself. When he says, "Be joyful in hope; patient in affliction; faithful in prayer," that is for the individual in the church, but every one of those things will help to bring harmony with all the others. So we are to live in harmony with one another, to be the kind of person who can be that and who will bring harmony to the fellowship rather than destroy it.

Which brings me to the *don't*. There is a false conceit that can come into a church whether it is social conceit or even

177

spiritual conceit. So he says first: associate with people of low position. If you are not careful, you can associate in church with people of your own set, your own social standing. It is particularly important that you associate in a church with those that others might not be willing to associate with. It is good for you too, and good for the whole body. Above all, again he mentions arrogance. This is the enemy of harmony. Anybody who is proud, anybody who is arrogant.... You cannot think highly of yourself without thinking lower about someone else. You can't be proud without being arrogant, so it is important for the harmony of the fellowship that we don't allow any trace of pride or arrogance. Those bullets all find my heart. I don't know about you, but at some point one of those bullets will penetrate your heart and make you think, "What am I doing" and "What shouldn't I be doing?"

In relation to outsiders, Paul has already slipped in one bullet already. I don't know if you noticed. "Bless those who persecute you and do not curse." I hope that refers to outsiders – it would be tragic if it referred to fellow Christians, but I have to tell you that one of the hardest things to bear is opposition from Christians. You don't expect it and it hurts. I think of my autobiography *Not as Bad as the Truth*, and I didn't choose that title, God did. I will tell you how and why. By the way, I thought anybody who wrote an autobiography was a supreme egotist. The only reason I did was because another publisher was approaching someone else to write my biography, and I was not having anybody else write it so I wrote it myself in self-defence.

Some years ago someone in Wales (I managed to track it down) started circulating rumours about me and my ministry which were outright lies. One was that I had stopped reading my Bible since I got filled with the Spirit. Ludicrous! I never read the Bible more than when I was filled with the Spirit. There were three such lies, which spread so rapidly.

You know what the Christian bush telegraph is like. These lies spread so quickly that I began to get letters cancelling speaking engagements. None of them would ever tell me what was wrong. They just said, "We're very sorry to tell you that arrangements for your visit have fallen through." I knew what was going on. I knew why they were cancelling. It was not only painful personally, it was even more painful to my wife, but more than that. I said, "Lord, it's affecting my ministry. These lies are closing doors to me." I really complained to the Lord quite loudly.

The Lord said to me, "David, the worst they can say about you is not as bad as the truth." And I thought, "Well, thank God they don't know the truth!" I went into the kitchen and told my wife what the Lord had said, because wives know the worst as well. Well, that's what the Lord said to me. He did add later, "I know the worst, and I still love you and use you." That was good enough for me. It cured all reaction to criticism from then on. I determined then that if ever I had to write my life story, it would be called *Not as Bad as the Truth*. That is how it came to be.

We can expect hostility from outside and ought to be ready to have the right reaction to it. You don't expect it from inside, but I am afraid it sometimes comes from inside people. Alas, once pastors become professional they are subject to the temptation to professional jealousy and then it can creep in. "He has got a bigger church than I have." It is amazing how it can creep in if you are not careful – but as to hostility, you should expect it from the outsider. We no longer fit. We are citizens of heaven now. We are misfits socially and spiritually with a world that has gone crazy. Therefore, you can expect that the better your church is in quality, the more trouble you can expect from outside. There are many who know the truth of that. Governments can be against you. Society can be against you. How do we deal with that?

Well, there's a *do* and a *don't* here and I am going to take the *don't* first. It is: retaliation; revenge. Don't try to get your own back – leave it to God. There is a thing called vengeance in God which is not a hateful thing, but it is a very certain thing. God will repay. On the day when God settles accounts, everybody who has been against the church will pay. They will be faced with an account that God has kept. So you don't need to retaliate. You don't need to get your own back. God will do it, and that is the secret of curing revenge. It is instinctive in human nature to give as good as you get, but leave it to God. Human revenge is not in place in the church, only divine vengeance. It is safe in God's hands. He will repay.

Now the *do* here is to work for reconciliation insofar as it depends on you. You will fail to be reconciled with some of your enemies. That is not your business. You can't help that, but insofar as it lies with you, be at peace with all of them. Don't let any trace of bitterness or resentment get in. Furthermore, you can do more than that. You can heap coals of fire on their head. That is something you can and should do, making them feel thoroughly embarrassed and ashamed. How do you do these things to your enemies? You pray for those who curse you, and you do good to those who do evil to you. That is the reaction of churches under severe hostility. That is the divine reaction. That is the way to deal with your enemies.

I remember a young man in the forces when I was a chaplain with the Royal Air Force. One night he was in a barrack room with others, and the first night he knelt down by his bed. The sergeant saw him praying and picked up his heavy, hobnail boots, and he threw a boot at this man, which caught his ear and cut it. Then he threw the other boot and that really hurt him badly, but he went on praying. The next morning the sergeant woke up and found the boots back at the foot of his bed, polished by the Christian. He didn't have to polish his own boots that morning. The man he had hurt with those boots the night before had polished them and put them back at his bunk. That is what Paul is talking about. It had a profound effect on that sergeant. It heaped coals of fire on his head. It is a lovely way to treat your enemies.

We have dealt with our relationships with God and our relationships with other people. Now Paul moves on to the relationships of Christians with their governments. Church and state relationships are important and were particularly so in Rome. The church was under the shadow of the Imperial government and Rome was not a democracy. It was more like an autocracy, government by one man, or an oligarchy, a group of men – the Senate in Rome's case. Here was a new church in Rome itself, under the shadow of an imperial government. It was vital that Christians should understand the right relationship with the state. So here we have one of the most political sections of the letter and Paul's clear commands to Christians as to their attitude to the state, whether it is democratic or a dictatorship. That is important. There is always a limit to our duty to the state. The limit is if the state ever tells us to do something that God has told us not to do, or if the state tells us not to do something that God has told us to do – then the text for that situation is found in Acts: we must obey God rather than man. That comes down the road after a lot of positive things. Peter, in his letter, teaches: Don't suffer for being a bad citizen; suffer for the right reason. Don't suffer for being a criminal whatever you do. That is bad witness, bad testimony.

There are two pressures on us from the state. One is the pressure of the state's authority, and the other is the pressure of the state's morality. We are to accept the one and reject the other. I am glad he includes both because the state has a morality as well as individuals. When the state of Rome was still a republic it was not too bad, but when it became an empire and the Roman governor became an emperor, from then on the state's morality went down. Of the first fifteen Roman emperors, fourteen were openly homosexual, for example, to say nothing of the corruption that brought.

Let us look first at the authority of government. They are described, whatever their nature, as the ministers of God, appointed by God. That is what I call the civic dignity. They are servants of God whether they know it or not. God has appointed governments to prevent anarchy. It is his gift to the world to give governments who put limits on what citizens can do. They are therefore ministers of God. When our Queen is crowned she is given a Bible and told that this is the royal law. Those are the words used. She is reminded that this is the law for her. I thank God we have a Queen who has understood that. She told Billy Graham that she knows exactly what it is to be born again. You may have noticed she has become steadily more Christian in her recent annual Christmas broadcasts. I am grateful for that, but supposing she wasn't? King Charles isn't, or when he becomes King Charles we will have a king who isn't Christian. He had the chance. He was prepared for confirmation by John Stott, who is dead now, but was a chaplain to the royal family at the time. When Charles was a boy he went "walkabout" in Australia when he was sent to a school there. On one of his Sunday walkabouts he found himself outside a tin hut in which a Pentecostal aboriginal congregation was meeting. He wandered in for the service and wrote home to the queen, "Dear Mother, if this was early Christianity I can understand how it spread." So he knows, but then he got in with a South African mentor who muddled him up greatly. Now he is advocating Islam.

But even so, God appoints governments. God has a casting vote in every election. He either gives us the government we deserve or the government we need, depending on whether he votes in justice or mercy. God revealed to me in Israel that Margaret Thatcher would be his choice. I wrote and told her: "I want to be the first in the country to congratulate you on becoming Prime Minister, because God has chosen you for the next election." She quoted from my letter in the first broadcast after her appointment, and it gave me an open door to her. Not that God is conservative, because when I was in Australia I saw a leading trade unionist's photograph on a newsagent's bookstall – a man called Bob Hawke. As I looked at his photograph, the Lord said, "He's my choice for Australia's prime minister." I began to ask churches to pray for Bob Hawke – because he's going to be your prime minister and you'll have to pray for him then. Pray for him now. I really got some stick from Christians. They said, "How dare you ask us to pray for that womaniser." I said, "But he's going to be your prime minister." They began to pray for him and he turned out to be a very much better prime minister than they expected. Strangely, in a dictatorship, we find it easy to believe that God can change one man for another one man, but in a general election we seem to lose that faith and think that he has no say in it. I know from personal experience that he has, so pray that he may vote in mercy and give you the government you need, or he can vote in justice and give you the government you deserve. He can control a democratic election. He is the God of history. He is the God of nations, not just of individuals. So get it clear that whatever the government you are under, that is God's establishment to restrain wickedness and to commend goodness. Those are the two functions of every government. God will hold them to account for whether they have commended goodness and condemned badness. They are his servant, his provision, his protection for our good, because God knows that anarchy will bring out the worst of sinful human nature. No government at all is a good deal worse than the worst government.

The Bible is not in favour of democracy. I have heard preachers say that. Cecil B. DeMille said it in the opening of the film *The Ten Commandments*. He said, "This film is about how democracy began." Democracy? Sinai? Never! We are not made for a democracy. We are not made to govern ourselves. We are made to live in a kingdom, but we don't want to live in a kingdom because there are so many bad kings. Even the good ones become corrupt when they get power. So, as Winston Churchill said, "Democracy is the worst possible form of government except all the others." That is a profound remark because in a democracy at least the people have the power to get rid of the government every few years. That is a privilege we ought to value.

Nevertheless, as one great British politician said, "A general election is one lot of sinners out and another lot in." I'm afraid that is the truth, but the government is God's provision for at least a limit on the bad things that citizens want to do. It is by his establishment. Therefore the punishment that is the sanction of all governments is of divine origin, or as Paul puts it here, "He does not bear the sword in vain." A government must use force against evil. A sword is not used to spank people, it is used to kill them, and this is God's sanction for the use of physical force by governments. How they use that, they will answer to him for. It is one of the church's functions to remind governments that they are accountable to God himself because he put them there, whatever form they take.

So both the establishment and the punishment of the state is of divine origin. Therefore, civilian duty is laid on Christians. That duty consists of two things: submit and support. They are God's authority in your country, and therefore you submit to them as good citizens unless they are telling you to do something God has told you not to do, or have told you not to do something God has told you to do. It is at that point that you have to say with the early disciples: we must obey God, rather than man. That is the point at which a Christian does rebel. I don't think a Christian joins in general rebellion or revolution, because so often human revolutions produce something worse than there was before. But it does mean there comes a point where a Christian will go to prison or die rather than disobey God. Happy will he be if the government recognises his conscience in this matter. Some do, but some don't. Christians are paying the price for that.

Do you know that the record is such today that up to a quarter of a million Christians die for their faith every year? I have to add that a great deal of that is in Muslim-controlled countries, but not exclusively. We need to remember our brethren who are paying the supreme price for their disobedience to the state and their obedience to God. You have got to go a long way up to that point in supporting the government and therefore we can affirm one more thing about submission. Paul is teaching this: Don't submit out of cowardice; submit out of conscience. What he means is that you can submit to the government out of fear of punishment. Take a simple example. As a driver you can choose to break the speed limit, or you can keep it, out of fear of being disqualified from driving. That is good enough for the world, but not good enough for the Christian. The Christian does it out of conscience.

One of my best friends in the world is called Peter, a retired second-hand car dealer in Australia. He was known in the whole of Australia as an honest car dealer. If you wanted the right price for a secondhand car, you would go to Peter. He sold a secondhand car every ninety seconds on Tuesdays and Thursdays in the home town where he lives. That man came to be a Christian through my tape recordings and he distributed hundreds of thousands of those recordings all over Australia, and even got them into Burma. He spread my word around the world because he wanted everybody to know the truth. I can tell you so many lovely stories, but he had a very high-powered Mercedes car. When he drove me around Australia in it I couldn't help but notice that it only did 29 mph in town and only 49 mph when he was out in the bush. When he was 500 miles from the nearest policeman it would still only do 49 mph. I couldn't help commenting because I knew the power of the engine in front of us. He simply said to me when I made a comment, "But David, isn't that holiness? How can I expect the angels to protect me when I am breaking a law made for my protection?" Now there was a man who kept the speed limit, not out of fear of losing his licence but out of conscience. Do you see the difference? Paul is teaching this: Don't keep the law out of fear of punishment from the law, do it out of conscience. Do it because you are told from the inside that you should be keeping the law, not from the outside. So that is submitting to the authority of government.

Now let us look at the matter of support. Two things are mentioned and the first is revenue, taxes. There must be tax. It costs money to have a government. They can't do anything without money from the public. Now comes the rub. Paul simply says, "A Christian submits to the government by paying the tax." No escaping that; no evasion of tax, however clever your accountant may be. I remember in Australia going to speak to the government in Canberra. The man who drove me to the airport in Melbourne was a pastor, and he kept me so busy with questions all the way that he went slower and slower. I said, "I'm speaking to the government tomorrow morning and I'm going to miss that plane to Canberra if you don't hurry up."

He just replied, "Well, I've just a few more questions to ask you," and he went even slower. The result was that I caught the plane, but my luggage didn't. I arrived in Canberra to speak to the government in my old clothes that I travel in. Can you imagine? Anyway, I spoke to the members of both houses together, which was a great privilege, but I will never forget one member of Parliament who shook my hand at the doors. Leaving, he just said, "David, I'm going home to rewrite my income tax returns." I wanted to shout, "Hallelujah!" Heaven was shouting because, "If one sinner repents, heaven has a celebration." I am quoting Jesus. That was a man really repenting. We are to fill out our income tax returns properly. Now this creates a real problem in some countries. I was in one country which I won't name, but everybody there is on the fiddle with their tax. The government knows this, and so they overcharge taxes to cover themselves against all the fiddling that is going on. Thus, if a Christian properly fills in their income tax they will have to pay far more than they should. An honest citizen is going to have to pay for that deficit. I had Christian businessmen asking me the very deep question, "What should I do? Because I know the government is allowing for fiddling and it is going to charge me more than they should charge me and expect me to fiddle it. Then they are content with the level."

I replied, "I'm not going to tell you, but you ask the Lord what you should do." There were businessmen who said, "I know if I pay the proper, full tax that they ask, I'll go out of business." He thankfully decided to do that and would rather go out of business, which actually he didn't. The Lord enabled him to make it up in amazing ways. That is the kind of tricky question you can get into when you are a Christian. There is, of course, a difference between legitimate tax avoidance and tax evasion. I am aware of that difference, but it is something of a blurred line between the two. Paul clearly teaches that a Christian pays his tax and supports the government financially.

There is another way you support the government, and it is as important as revenue. This is respect. That is a very interesting point to put in. One of the ways you can bring down a government is to ridicule them, to kill respect. If there is one thing absent in current society in so many countries, it is the absence of respect. I am talking about the Western world as well as other countries. All the Ten Commandments are based on respect: respect your parents; respect human life; respect other people's properties; respect the truth about other people. The Ten Commandments begin with respect for God, for his name, for his day. It is all there. God gave us those commandments because he knows that a society collapses when respect is lost. In my country there is a generation growing up that has lost respect for parents, the police and politicians. There have been some wicked comic programs about politicians on our television in which constantly making fun of the powers that are over us has reduced their status in people's eyes. So respect as well as revenue is due to whatever government is over you, whether it is your party or not. You are careful as a Christian not to destroy respect by ridicule.

So much for the authority of the state. Up to a certain point, conformity is the Christian duty – up to that point but no further. The state also has a morality. For example, our state government has now legislated for same-sex marriage. At the moment, churches are excused if they have a conscience about it, but the day will follow when churches are made subject to that law, and if we don't marry two women or two men together we shall face penalty. The morality of the state is not to be conformed to. The morality of the society that the state produces is not to be conformed to.

So Paul now looks at nonconformity. The first thing he mentions is debt. I have been challenging congregations in England about debt. According to my New Testament, to owe anybody anything is a sin. I have checked up with average evangelical congregations and I have asked them, "How many of you are in debt?" The usual show of hands is two-thirds. Their preachers have never told them that a Christian doesn't get into debt, but then we live in a credit society. Everybody so easily builds up a debt, especially if they take out a mortgage for a house they really can't afford if the interest rates go up. That's one of the easiest traps to get into debt. I do want to make it absolutely clear that taking out a mortgage on your house is not a debt. To get into debt with a mortgage is to get behind with your repayments. That is debt. There are two ways of stealing money. One is to take money from people, and the other is to withhold money that is due to them which they have every right to have from you. You withhold it because you haven't got it to pay. That is debt. You can have a proper business arrangement of a loan and that is a valid business, but if you get behind with repayments and therefore are preventing money that belongs to your creditor being paid, then you are in debt. Paul says owe no man anything.

My great-grandfather was a grocer in a town in the north of England. Every Saturday night he went down the street, into the butcher, into the baker, each shop, paying off whatever money he owed them. He became a byword, a joke, in the place where he lived. People could set their clocks by him. "There's Pawson, off to pay his debts," because he would not go to church on a Sunday to worship God with a debt hanging over him. Things have changed a bit since then. So, owe no man anything. That refers to monetary debts which you are behind in paying or repaying. We have a moral debt also. We are to fulfil the law. To be in debt is to steal, and stealing is against the law of God and of men. So, no monetary debts and no moral debts; we owe it to our society to fulfil our payment of all debts. The moral debt is to love them. You don't steal from people if you love them. Love is the fulfilling of the law. You don't damage their reputation if you love them.

Not only does the Christian fulfil the law of the land and of the Lord at the same time by keeping out of debt, but the other aspect that Paul concentrates on now is quite a big surprise, and that is understanding the time. It is a strange thing to say, but in our attitudes to the state and society, we are to understand the time. That is going to help us enormously. What time is it on God's clock? Where are we in God's purpose for history, in what he's doing for the nations? Understand the time, and in a very practical, down-to-earth way, Paul says, "Wake up!" It is time for Christians to wake up. It was the next few verses a child was reading aloud who was overheard by Saint Augustine. That philosopher, already with a mistress and an illegitimate son, heard that wake-up call to understand the time and therefore to live by the time. There is an alarm here. Wake up! The night is far gone. The day is at hand. That is the time clock that all Christians of all generations need to live by – wake-up time, not sleepy-time.

The next thing was: and get dressed. Dress yourselves by putting off the deeds of darkness and by putting on the armour of light. The two sides to getting dressed properly are to get some things off and other things put on. Christians, as citizens of the state, understand the time – that we are in the last human age of history, that it is wake-up time, and get dressed in the right way: put on the armour of light. It is a very spiritual ending to a practical chapter, but it fits. You will be the best citizen of your country if you understand the time in which we live, that earthly governments have a time limit on them, and that the world is passing away. That gives you a healthy attitude to a government that is here today and gone tomorrow, be it election time or between elections. There is still always this wake-up call. These few verses of Romans so hit Augustine, as a young philosopher who had gone astray quite badly, that he became Saint Augustine and bishop of the church in North Africa. It gives you an eternal perspective of things that are temporal. Every government is temporary, and it will change for another, one way or another. It is the government of God that will not change; it is the kingdom of God, the kingdom of light, the kingdom of the day. Time and again Paul says this in other letters too, notably Thessalonians: We are not as those who are sleepy of the night. We are people of the day, of the light; we have woken up, and we are getting dressed in the right way for eternity. That gives you that essential eternal dimension to the way we behave, even as citizens today in our contemporary world.

7. MORE RELATIONSHIPS

ROMANS 14:1–16:27

```
A  STRONG AND WEAK (14:1-15:7)
      1. DISPUTABLE MATTERS (14:1-12)
            a. Examples
                  i. Diet (vegetarianism)  ii. Day (sabbatarianism)
            b. Exhortation
                  i. Not accusing others  ii. But accounting ourselves
      2. DISARMING MANNERS (14:13-15:7)
            a. Consideration
                  i. Not food or drink for the body
                  ii. But righteousness, peace and joy in the Spirit
            b. Edification
                  i. Not to break down  ii. But to build up
            c. Discretion
                  i. Not faithless sin  ii. But faithful silence
            d. Imitation
                  i. Not to please ourselves  ii. But to accept others
B  JEW AND GENTILE (15:8-33)
      1. CHRIST – servant to the Jews (8-13)
            a. To confirm the promises  b. To convert the Gentiles
      2. PAUL – priest to the Gentiles (14-33)
            a. East – already done
                  i. How?  Word, deed, sign
                  ii. Where?  Jerusalem to Illyzicum
            b. West – yet to do
                  i. Rome, then Spain  ii. Jerusalem, then Rome
C  NEAR AND FAR (16:1-24)
      1. GREETINGS TO (1-16)
            a. Women  b. Relatives  c. Colleagues
      2. WARNINGS ABOUT (17-20)
            a. Division  b. Deception  c. Deflection
      3. GREETINGS FROM (21-24)
            a. Colleagues  b. Relatives  c. Officials
DOXOLOGY (25-27) God is:
                        able    )
                        open    )    to Him be the glory
                        wise    )
```

PLEASE READ ROMANS 14:1–16:27

The last three chapters of Romans (14–16) tell us more about relationships. Now relationships within a fellowship are most acutely in tension when Jews and Gentile believers are meeting together. There are tensions that arise out of scruples, which are hesitations people have because of their conscience, their culture or their traditional upbringing. We all have them. There are differences that Paul calls disputable issues, and he means that they are debatable – matters not dealt with directly in scripture and therefore without any clear biblical guidance but which different people believe to be right or wrong.

Let us consider some illustrations. I was ordained a Methodist minister back in the 1950s, and in those days Methodism in Britain made teetotalism a principle. I had to promise, as a Methodist pastor, never to touch alcohol. The Methodists of Britain in those days (they have relaxed it now) were all strongly anti-drink. The Methodist church in Norway was somewhat different. They had the same attitude to smoking, and anybody who smoked was considered a really bad sinner. The president of the English Methodist church, as soon as he was out of the pulpit, stuck a pipe in his mouth, and he was an inveterate pipe smoker. He went on an official visit to the Methodists of Norway, and he horrified them all by sticking his pipe into his mouth. When the president of the Methodist church in Norway visited Britain on an official visit, the opposite applied. He happily took a drink in moderation. That is a typical example of a disputable issue.

There are many others. Should women wear make-up? On the whole, American women seem to have no inhibition, but I have been to other parts of the world where that is considered extremely sinful. I have two rings. They are both gold, because gold is a metal that doesn't tarnish or rust. I have my name on both in Hebrew. One was given to me on the eighth day of the Feast of Tabernacles, which as you know is the wedding day when they marry the law for another year. I watched a Jew make it for me in a little shop in Jerusalem. Our twenty-fifth wedding anniversary fell on the eighth day of the Feast of Tabernacles and we celebrated it with twelve hundred Christians in the wilderness of Judea late at night with a great pillar of fire, a bonfire. We ate roast quail, and it was a wonderful anniversary. My wife gave me that ring which has my name in Hebrew – on the walls of Jerusalem. She said, "I want you to be a watchman on the wall," so I like wearing that ring which is not just a wedding ring.

The other ring was owned by a Jew many, many years ago and it has my name on it in Hebrew, this time the other way round. It reads left to right. Why? It is a signet ring, to press into wax. They were building a big new block in London, and found that in digging the foundations they were digging through a very old Jewish cemetery. Among the bones they found this ring owned by a Jew called David and they gave it to me. I was very grateful for it. I said, "I'll wear that till I die and beyond." I want to be buried in those two rings, but I went to Romania where one of the biggest sins (Christians consider) is to wear a gold ring. I can't get them off, so as soon as I began my first preach there I explained why I wore them. It is for the love of Israel in my heart.

So Christians have different scruples depending on their conscience and their culture. When I first went to India to Hyderabad for a Christian event we went into a huge convention building that had no seats, just a bare concrete floor. As we went in, all the people took off their sandals, mostly plastic flip-flops, and just threw them into a pile at the door and then went in, in either bare feet or stockinged feet. That is their culture. Well, I had a nice, new pair of sandals on and I thought: when they come out they just pick up a pair of sandals from the top of the heap and go off with them. I'm afraid I hid my sandals round the corner, but I took them off to go in and worship with them. That is their scruple. In many countries you take your shoes off when you go into a house. In Britain we usually don't. We can develop these traditions and they get right into the church. Some countries I go to would be horrified that congregations are sitting with male and female side by side. In every service they sit with all the women on one side and all the men on the other. When I used to go to Communist countries that was invariably the pattern. They would be horrified that we mix the sexes when we worship God.

This is the kind of disputable issue that Paul is dealing with, when you can have strong convictions either way. When these come together in the same fellowship, you have got a problem. This particularly applies in a fellowship of Jews and Gentile believers together. Paul's whole letter is about this tension, in which the Gentiles of the Roman church were having difficulty welcoming the Jewish believers back again under Nero (after Claudius had sent them away from the city). Paul is dealing with that and he now deals with the very practical side of it. The two issues which he calls disputable are *diet* and *days*. Of course, in this case, the Jewish culture has much stronger convictions than the Gentile culture.

Kosher food is a very strong thing with the Jewish culture. There was the added problem of the fact that most meat available in Rome had been offered to the gods before it was sold. The question was: was the meat offered to idols? Christian can't eat that. So there was a difference of opinion on diet, in this case around vegetarianism. There are Christian vegetarians today who don't seem convinced by Genesis 9, where God gave permission to us to eat meat, which has not been rescinded. Nevertheless, there are Christians who genuinely believe that Christians should not eat animals that have been killed for their consumption. So vegetarian food is such an issue.

The other issue was special days. For the Jew, the Sabbath Saturday is a special day. Some Christians have thought that it has now been changed and the Christian Sabbath is on Sunday, the day of the resurrection. They have a Sabbatarian attitude to Sunday. I was brought up in a godly family. Sunday was the Sabbath to them, therefore I was not allowed to use a bicycle or a camera on Sunday. This became a sinful thing. It caused quite a crisis when I went away to work on the farm and the nearest church was five miles away. I had to ride a bicycle from the farm to the church just to attend worship. The first time I got on a bicycle on Sunday, my background made me face up to that. Am I free to ride a bike on Sunday? I came to the conclusion after studying the Bible that, yes, of course I am. I had to get over that scruple.

This is the kind of thing we are talking about. The Jewish scruples were first of all, on food, diet, and secondly, on special days, particularly the Sabbath, that weekly day that was devoted to the God of Israel. The Jewish identity during all the two thousand years they have been away from their land are circumcision, kosher food, and the Sabbath. They have kept up those three basic things wherever they were, and that is part of the miracle of their survival. Even to this day, Jewish believers in Jesus have cultural scruples. There are certain things they don't feel comfortable doing.

How do we deal with a fellowship in which there are strong Christians and weak Christians? The first thing is that we are going to have two surprises here. The first surprise is that the strong Christians are the ones who feel free to do things, and the weak Christians are those who have scruples about doing certain things. A sign of a strong Christian is someone who has matured. The conscience is like a moral compass. We are all born with a moral compass called a conscience, but it is conditioned by our upbringing. It doesn't point to true north; mind you, no compass ever did. The true magnetic north moves around. With an aircraft's compass, they have to allow for the fact that it is not pointing to the North Pole. We assume every compass points to the North Pole but it doesn't. The magnetic north moves around. As the compass is not reliable for true north, your conscience is not reliable for true morality. It is approximate, depending on your upbringing. Things you were brought up to believe were wrong, that compass in you will point to. Part of maturing as a Christian is adjusting that compass to true north, to the will of God and to what God has said is right and wrong. That can take quite a lot of adjustment. I had to learn to ride a bicycle on Sunday as part of that adjustment. A mature Christian is much freer than a Christian with a lot of scruples from upbringing or culture and background.

Have I explained this enough for you to realise what Paul is dealing with? Christians can have very strong convictions because their compass has not been fully adjusted yet to God's will. It is still to a degree conditioned by background, upbringing, and so on. So if you were brought up in a church that said Christians don't go to the cinema, that will be part of your compass. You may mature and feel free to go to the cinema, but you will, if you mature, decide which films you should see. Do you see what I mean? You are freer, but you have adjusted your compass.

So on these two disputable matters Paul is saying that the strong Christian is the one who is freer to do things than the weak Christian who has this carryover of scruples from background. The next thing surprising to us is not who is the strong Christian and who is the weak Christian, but who has to do the adjusting. Now you think Paul would say the weak Christian with scruples must adjust their lifestyle to the strong Christian who is more mature and freer to do these things, but in fact he says the opposite. All of his teaching now is addressed to the strong Christian, to adjust his behaviour to the weak Christian. Now get that shock into your mind, because it is a shock. If you are not careful you can damage a weak brother because you override his scruples. In other words, it is the strong brother who is free to do a thing who is also free not to do it for the sake of his weaker brother. That is the point I am trying to get across. It is a bit of a shock to some Christians that Paul expects the strong to adapt to the weak for the sake of harmony within the fellowship.

I have mentioned the two things he mentions: vegetarianism and Sabbatarianism. Still to this day in England, Sunday observance is an issue among some Christians. Some years ago we had a big campaign by some Christians called "Keep Sunday Special". Many of the arguments that those who backed that campaign were using were arguments for the Sabbath and Sabbatarianism. Christians are free from the Sabbath law. The fourth commandment is not applied in the new covenant, but it is often appealed to in the name of keeping Sunday special. At the time, I naughtily wrote an article in a national Christian magazine and entitled it, "Keep Monday Special," and pointed out the Scriptural teaching. We are not bound by the Sabbath law of Moses any more than we are bound by the tithing law of Moses, though more churches try to apply that to Christians and force them to tithe to the church, which of course ensures a good income for the church, but it is not biblical.

I have read a very funny book entitled *The Year of Living Biblically*. It was written by a Jewish reporter in

New York. Although he was married to a Jewess and he was circumcised, he was not practising. He decided as a journalistic experiment to live by the Bible for twelve months and report on what happened. It really is the funniest book you will read. He was deadly serious. He had to abandon most of his clothes because they were mixed material. He discarded most of his suits and wore a cotton nightdress virtually, to the embarrassment of his whole family, but at least it was one material. Remember this was in New York, and (if ladies will excuse this) I think the funniest was about the Mosaic law that you must be very careful not to have contact with a woman who is in her monthly bleeding period. He came home one night, and he knew his wife was in her monthly period. He was about to sit down in the easy chair by the fire, and she said, "I have sat in that chair this morning." So he jumped up, and moved to another chair, and she said, "I've sat in that chair too." She had deliberately sat in every chair in the house and the poor man couldn't sit down that night.

This is how the book goes on, but he literally tried to do everything Moses had said and everything that Jesus had said. He agreed that was in the Bible, and therefore he was going to live biblically for twelve months. He just got into such a muddle and such scrapes. The conclusions he came to at the end of twelve months were first that it is quite impossible, and second, that it is a good deal harder to live by the New Testament commands than those in the Old Testament. That is a very interesting conclusion.

These are matters of scruples now. Even a Jew who has come into the new covenant is now free from the law of Moses, but one of the most difficult questions that Israeli believers are facing, and the fellowships of Israeli believers are almost at war over this, is how much of the Mosaic covenant they should keep. They know they are free from it, but somehow they have got a lot of scruples in the new covenant from the old covenant. By the way, the Old Testament is not the old covenant. The old covenant is the Mosaic covenant. The Noahic covenant, the Abrahamic, the Davidic covenants all come straight over into the new. They are not the old. The new covenant has only replaced Moses and his law.

I can understand the tension that is arising among Israeli believers these days in Israel. They are not quite sure. They meet on the Saturday, if they can, rather than Sunday. That is part of their belief. There are Christians who believe that Christians should observe the Sabbath law. They are called the Seventh Day Adventists. They begin their worship at six o'clock on Friday evening. I am afraid I find many Christians, particularly Zionists today, believe that all Christians should be becoming Jewish. They therefore observe the Jewish Sabbath in a Christian-Gentile home.

These are all the issues of scruples, disputable issues, and so the exhortation to the strong follows the examples that Paul gives. The exhortation is: "Don't accuse others." That applies only to disputable issues. Don't accuse them of sinning; don't judge them, but realise that you will give account for yourself, not them. They are doing it to the Lord, and though their conscience is not yet mature and therefore freer, nevertheless, they are doing it to the Lord. It is their conviction, and the strong who is free not to do that should not judge them and should not condemn them and not look down on them. God is their judge, and we should only be accountable to God for ourselves in disputable issues. That is very good advice.

Paul goes on to use a phrase again and again – "to the Lord" – especially when he is dealing with Sabbatarianism, or turning Sunday into a Sabbath. If you want to know the new covenant fulfilment of the Sabbath, it is resting from your own works every day of the week. Paul says in a fellowship there are some who believe that one day is special to the Lord, and others believe that every day is to the Lord. There is a tension. Don't judge each other. Just make sure that you are convinced in your own mind and that you are responsible to the Lord. It is he who should have the last word in such disputes. When we answer to the Lord on the Day of Judgment we won't answer for anyone else, just ourselves. We need constantly to remember that.

He now turns to a section which I label "Disarming Manners". Your *attitudes* are going to make all the difference in this. Things can so easily become arguments, even splits. I have known churches split over dancing, make-up and cinema. It is tragic when believers split over scruples, where some conscientiously hold to the law in their own convinced minds and others are free to do otherwise. It is a question of etiquette. There is such a thing as godly manners in a fellowship where there are such tensions. There are four things in particular that Paul says should mark the strong and their manners towards the weak, those with more scruples. First, consideration: get a true perspective; get things in proportion. That is when he says, "For the kingdom is not a matter of food and drink." What goes into people's bodies is not a kingdom matter. Therefore arguments about teetotalism or moderate drinking are, in a sense, irrelevant to the kingdom.

What does matter in the kingdom is righteousness, peace and joy. Those are the important things in the kingdom. I want you to notice carefully the order. Righteousness first, then that brings peace, and then you have joy. The real crucial principles of the kingdom are really nothing to do with what you eat or drink. They are to do with your righteousness, your peace, and then your joy in the Holy Spirit. That is worth arguing about. That is important, so get a true perspective.

Don't get things out of perspective. Don't enlarge a thing beyond its relative unimportance. That is what he means by consideration. By the way, that is the only mention of the word "kingdom" in the whole letter. Those who think this is the gospel Paul preached need to think again. He preached the kingdom, but that is the only verse that mentions it in connection with scruples.

The next thing is *edification*. The word "edifice" means building, and edification is to build people up, not to break them down. We are not in the business of demolition. We are in the business of edification. Paul made a lot of that in 1 Corinthians 14. He taught that when you go to church, your first consideration is not expressing yourself but edifying those around you. What you do in a church should build them up and not break them down. I am afraid I get a bit allergic to worship leaders who say, "Now each of you do your own thing. If you want to sit, you sit. If you want to stand, you stand. If you want to kneel, you kneel." That is breaking up a congregation.

When our children were little there was a ritual which they did faithfully once every year. At an ungodly hour in the morning, they would come and stand at the foot of my bed in a straight row and sing to me: "Happy birthday to you". After singing, they would then present me with a bag of their favourite sweets. Now you could say, "Wouldn't you rather, as a father, that they came to you separately and said, 'I love you?'" No, in standing in a row together and singing together, they were acknowledging that they were a family. Doing a thing together, doing the same thing together, having a ritual together and singing to the Father together – he may enjoy that more than a lot of people doing their own thing. When you go to church you do not go to express yourself, you go to edify the others, and therefore you don't do things that will puzzle people. You don't all speak in tongues.

That is not going to help everybody there. Therefore your consideration is now, "What should I be doing to help this person next to me?" Edification is a Christian duty – building people up. If you ride over the scruples of a weaker brother, you are destroying him. You are not building him up, you are breaking him down.

The next thing is *discretion*. You may be free to do something, and the weaker brother may copy you to his own harm, because he may be filled with doubts while he is doing it. He will do it because you are doing it, filled with doubt. Whatever is not of faith is sin. He is doing it out of conformity to you, not out of his faith. That is wrong, so you don't do it. You become discreet. You keep quiet about your convictions, and you simply adjust your behaviour to his. He may be the weaker brother, and you may be the stronger one, but it is up to the stronger to adjust to the weaker. Discretion is another disarming manner of the strong. Finally, there is *imitation*: imitate Christ. Paul quotes a text from the Old Testament, a Messianic text about Christ being willing to be insulted. In a sense, when you adapt to the weaker brother you are feeling you are insulting yourself. You are sitting on top of a conviction to be free, but you will do it to imitate Christ who bore our insults without complaining. Like Christ we are not to please ourselves.

I am afraid that we have got into a culture now in the West and it is spreading to other parts of the world, where we are encouraged to express ourselves, to release ourselves, to concentrate on what "I" think. Many of the choruses we sing were written for private devotion. They are 'I' songs. You know Jesus said when you want personal prayer, go into a room, shut the door, and say, "Our Father...." There is really no such thing as private prayer. You are part of a body the world over that is praying, and what you are praying about, somebody else is praying about. Even in private, say

"Our Father". Corporate prayer is the normal prayer for a Christian, but there are so many new songs which are "I" and "me" and "my" and how I feel about the Lord and how he feels about me. It worries me. It is part of the individualism of the 1980s that is still hanging around. We are a corporate people. Most of our songs should be "our", "we".

This is about a bee in my bonnet, but we need to think of what we are singing. I can't sing the feelings of somebody else if I don't have them, but many of the great hymns of Charles Wesley, who wrote 6,000 hymns, were packed with scripture and were corporate songs. He did write one or two individual songs, and alas, they are the ones that everybody sings today – like, "Long my imprisoned spirit lay, fast bound in sin and nature's night; thine eye diffused a quick'ning ray, I rose, the chains fell off; my heart was free." That was his personal experience, but most of his songs are "our" songs, corporate songs, in which we can all join together and share the same thoughts.

So imitate Christ, and his conclusion is: so the strong should bear the weak. The strong, who is free to do things, should carry the burden of those who don't feel free to do the same things. That was particularly relevant in Rome, so that the Gentile believers would accept the Jewish believers, but it is true of every fellowship.

In 15:8–33 we enter a section which is full of worship. The word "worship" occurs eleven times in one form or another in the next section. Paul is concerned about harmony in worship together, so that Jews and Gentiles will glorify God: v. 6, praise him; v. 7, glorify him, v. 9, praise him, sing to him, rejoice in him, v. 10, and praise him in the next verse – eleven times. He has put a vision before us of a church which has such harmony between the people that when they worship it is a corporate exercise of singing harmony, musical harmony – a harmonious sound to God.

That is the ultimate exercise, however he has a unique way of mentioning this. He points out what Gentiles owe to Jews, and we need to remember this.

Many years ago, some of us put up a huge tent in a London park in Finchley because nobody would lend us their building for what we wanted to do. We announced that in it we would have an evening for the Jewish people of Finchley. Finchley is almost a Jewish colony now. Most of the Jews who used to live in the poor east end of London had moved to the better-off Finchley area of northwest London. It was Margaret Thatcher's constituency. We put on a kosher supper for all the Jews who would come. About 1200 finally came, and then we had a meeting. I spoke, and a Jewish rabbi and I spoke on this subject: The time has come for Gentiles to repay their debt to the Jews.

Rabbi Hardman was the speaker, and at the end of the meeting he said to the whole meeting, "I was the first Jewish rabbi as a chaplain to the forces to enter Dachau concentration camp," one of the first camps to be released after World War II. He held up an enlarged photograph, of himself in army uniform as a Jewish chaplain – standing, looking down into a mass grave of Jews, in which thin skeletons were piled on top of each other. Then he said, "Tonight is the first night since then when I've had hope." It was most moving, and his hope was based on the fact that Christians had done this for the Jews in Finchley. The word of that meeting has gone around the entire Jewish world. Margaret Thatcher sent a special message to us, because it was in her constituency. To this day I still meet Jews who have heard of that meeting in which I simply said, "The time has come for Gentiles to repay their debt to the Jews." That one meeting has had an amazing effect. Recordings of it have gone round almost every synagogue. Somehow it was like pushing a plug into a socket and finding the socket was live when you pushed it in. It sent a shockwave. It has been widely known among Christians. That was in the early 1950s and still they talk about it. Three of us had got together and put on that meeting for Jews, in the heart of a Jewish area in London and cooked them a kosher meal. Now we could have said, "Christians are free to eat anything." Even Peter was told, "Rise and eat," and was told all foods are clean to the Christian. We could have emphasised that to them, but we didn't. We had laid on a kosher meal for them. It is an example of the strong adjusting to the weak, and it had that effect worldwide.

Now Paul makes two points that the Gentiles owe to Jews. The first point is that Christ was a servant to the Jews in Israel. When on two occasions he got outside Israel, he healed a Gadarene demoniac and a Syro-phoenician woman's child. He said to that woman, "It's not right to take food meant for the children and give it to dogs." He was testing her to see what faith she had. She came up with a brilliant retort: "But even the puppy dogs are allowed to eat the scraps that fall from the table." He realised what faith she had and healed her child – a wonderful incident. When he sent out the disciples they were to go to the lost sheep of the house of Israel. It looked as if Jesus came just for Jews. His ministry was limited to the Jews with a few rare exceptions, but at the end of his life he told his twelve Jewish disciples, "Now go and make disciples of all the ethnic groups [all the *ethne*, all the nations]." He sent them to the Gentile world. It still took Peter a long time to learn that, but he learned it. Then Paul, that Jewish Jew, was sent as an apostle to the Gentiles.

In other words, Jesus had the Gentiles in his heart all along. He came as a Jew to the Jews, but his objective was to fulfil the promises made to the patriarchs. God had promised Abraham that he would be the father of many nations and of kings of nations. Jesus came to fulfil that promise, but he did it by concentrating on Jews in his lifetime. Then after he rose from the dead he said: now go and share that with the whole world, to the uttermost parts of the earth; don't try to do it without the Holy Spirit power, but wait for that and then go to the uttermost parts of the earth and share it. That is how much Gentiles owe to the Jew, Jesus. Then Paul himself describes himself as a minister of Jesus Christ to the Gentiles.

So not only did Jesus come to confirm the promises to the Jews, but also his ultimate objective was to convert the Gentiles. Paul now shares his strategic mission to the Gentiles, and he is a Jew! The Gentiles he has led to the Lord owe him, a Jew, that he has brought them the liberating gospel. He then writes about what he has done and what he is yet to do. He had already done his mission in the east of the Mediterranean. He was going to do the the same west of the Mediterranean. His ambition was to preach where Christ was not known. Now he was known in the east of the Roman empire because Paul had done it. He didn't say "because I've done it" but was humble enough to say, "This is what the Lord has accomplished through me." It was the Lord's work through him.

Now he tells how he did it. Take special note of this. The three dimensions to his mission wherever he went are: word, deed, and sign. You can find all those carefully mentioned in Romans 15. That is true New Testament evangelism: preaching the word, practising the deed – doing good, yes, and, above all, signs and wonders. You are not into New Testament evangelism until you are doing all three. That makes a mighty impact. The real impact on the Muslim world will be through signs, particularly healing in the name of Jesus.

At one church I visited I was amazed. Almost the entire

congregation looked Muslim, mostly Arab or Pakistani. I said to the English pastor, "How on earth did you get all these?" Well, I asked him first, "Are they ex-Muslims?" He said, "Yes, almost every one of them."

So I asked, "How did you get them into church?"

He replied, "Well, we have a simple method. We have people in every street around here who tell us when a Muslim falls ill and calls the doctor. As soon as we hear that a Muslim is ill, we go and knock on the front door. We don't take Bibles. We don't take tracts. We just say to them, 'We've heard that someone here is sick. We'd like to come and pray for them if you would welcome that.' In every case, they welcome it. Before they go in, they say, 'We shall be praying to Isa [their name for Jesus] because he has the healing gift.' They say, 'Well, still come in, and you pray for the sick.' We go in, pray for the sick, they're healed, and then they're asking, 'Who was that that came to our house and healed our relative?' Then they start coming to our church."

The church meets in a former nightclub, and unfortunately they haven't redecorated it yet. You can guess what it looks like—black walls, red lights and all sorts of things. They have certainly removed some of the pictures, but I thought, "Here's an English pastor in an ex-nightclub," and it was obviously that, "and he's managed to fill a church with about 120 ex-Muslims." All he has done is this: "Can we come and pray for the sick?" He said no-one has refused yet. Then when they see the miracle, the sign, they come to church, and they hear the word.

I am convinced that an evangelism that is only word will not convert the Muslim or perhaps anybody else. It needs to be backed up by the deed, the way you live, and the sign that you are the servant of a supernatural God. I plead with you to consider this as New Testament evangelism: word, deed, and sign. Paul says, "I preach the word." "They saw my deeds." Even as a tentmaker they saw them, and the signs followed. That is what Jesus told us to do: Go and preach the word with signs following. Demonstrate the kingdom before you try to declare it. That is what Jesus said to the twelve when he sent them out two by two: Go into a town, demonstrate the kingdom, and then tell them the kingdom has come to their town. I think nothing short of signs and wonders will really have impact in the Muslim world.

Not only was this *how* he did it, but he then says *where* he did it — from Jerusalem to Illyricum, which is in the Balkans, on the eastern shores of the Aegean Sea. He told them that he had done the whole district. Now what was he doing in the district? The answer is very clear. His objective was to plant a church in the key city of an area or a state, and then leave, and leave that church to evangelise that whole region. That was his strategy – brilliant! So he was going on to Spain, to do the same in the western part of the Mediterranean empire that he had done in the east – plant a church in the key city, and they can do the rest. Don't try and do it all yourself! Plant a church in a key city, and leave them to do it. Leave them equipped to do it, but leave a church that can grow and spread by itself.

So, using that excellent missionary method Paul had planted churches in cities like Ephesus, Thessalonica, Athens and Corinth, then moved on and considered his work done. Amazing! But before going to the west of Rome, to Spain, there is another intervention. He says he is on his way to Jerusalem first, delivering money the Gentiles have given for Jewish believers who were suffering and needed help. That is an interesting little sidelight on the Jewish-Gentile issue.

Then he finishes by asking for their co-operation. He expects a struggle in Jerusalem and wanted his readers in Rome to join with him in praying that he might be delivered from the unbelieving Jews. He did not realise what that was going to mean, but when he got to Jerusalem it caused a Jewish riot from which he had to be rescued by Roman soldiers. He asked the Gentile believers in Rome also to pray that the Jewish believers in Jerusalem would welcome him, because that was a doubtful proposition. They had not welcomed Paul when he was first converted, they were very suspicious of him. They were even more troubled when he started bringing Gentiles in without circumcising them and without putting them under Moses' law. So there was a lot of suspicion of Paul – both from believing Jews and unbelieving Jews in Rome. So he asks the Gentile believers of Rome to join in praying that he would not have trouble with the unbelieving Jews and be delivered from them (as he was) and that he would also be welcomed by the believing Jews (as he was). Their prayers had a place in that.

Of course he was looking forward to coming and seeing the believers in Rome, wanting to "come, enjoy and be refreshed". Little did he dream he would come chained to a Roman soldier and be under house arrest; nevertheless, God brought him to Rome and fulfilled his ambition to visit that place. Of course, we don't know what happened at his first trial in Rome. Tradition said he was released and did manage to go further west in his mission, which may have happened. The book of Acts closes with his first trial. It is interesting that the book of Acts exactly parallels the Gospel of Luke. Of course, it had the same author. They were simply Volume 1 and Volume 2. Both begin with Mary. Both books begin with the disciples and then the first opposition. They go all the way through Jesus' life again, up to his trial. Then it stops. There is no account in Acts of the death of Paul. Up to then, the theme of Acts is in the Gospel – all that Jesus began to do and to teach; and he is now continuing with another body, the church.

I commend to you putting the two books together and

seeing how remarkably parallel they are. Jesus went through three trials; Paul went through three trials. In all cases the judges had to admit that Paul was innocent, as Pilate did with Jesus. It stops short of Paul going to his death, though he did. He was probably released from the first trial. The book of Acts was written for his judge. Both the gospel of Jesus in Luke and the book of Acts were written for one man. He tells us who the man was in both books. "The former treatise, O Theophilus, I wrote for you," and he calls him the most honourable, the title of a judge.

I think that while Doctor Luke was in Caesarea, while Paul was there, he wrote his Gospel about Jesus. Then, when he followed him to Rome, Paul was still in prison, but Luke wrote Acts. That is why you get such a long section at the end of Acts about the shipwreck in Malta. It is exactly the kind of detail that someone would include and even enlarge, to defend a man on trial for his life. Luke clearly wrote both books to defend Paul at his trial. So he was explaining for the judge, first of all, where this new religion of Christ began, and (his second volume) how Paul had come to be included. That is why there's more about Paul in Acts than about any of the other apostles – it is a defence of Paul.

The final defence of Paul is to say to the judge, "This man was shipwrecked. He saved the entire crew and he saved the soldiers guarding him." That is a good plea to a judge. It is almost as if Luke signs off Acts with the words, "The case rests, your Honour." He is defending Paul in both books. God must have been very pleased because he saw both books as part of his word. Without Acts and without Luke we would have lost so much. We would never have heard the parable of the good Samaritan or the parable of the prodigal son. Luke put these together as accurately as he could – as only a doctor could who was used to being accurate in diagnoses and reports. So this doctor wrote this for one man, Theophilus, one of Paul's judges at his first trial. Everything in those two books can be explained by their being briefs for the defence almost. Well, that is Paul: join me in my struggle.

Don't dismiss Chapter 16, to which we now turn. Many Christians have done so and say, "It's just a list of names and greetings – there is no message here." But there is a profound message. I am going to explain what it is all about. Now Paul is talking about the relationship between near and far, between Christians in one church and Christians in many churches. This is a wider relationship now. Some of the earliest manuscripts of Romans don't include chapter sixteen. Alas, some early Christians thought it had no message and therefore cut it off and said, "It's not relevant to today. We don't know any of these people personally, so what's the point of including that in the Word of God?" Fortunately, we have the full manuscript of what Paul did write, and it included chapter 16.

It is the longest list of greetings in the New Testament. Paul was used to giving greetings of two or three people at the end of a letter, but here there are far more, a whole chapter full. Most of them are Jews. When the Christian creed includes the phrase "I believe in the communion of the saints" it is pointing to this belief – that we not only need right relationships within our local church and its scruples and its different ethnic groups, we need relations with churches elsewhere. Paul prayed for churches he had never been to. He prayed for Christians he had never met. He had a wide network, and this final chapter tells us about it. A key to that wider network was greetings. I hope you are building a network that is wider than your own work. Our example is here.

There are three sections to this final chapter. The first section is Paul asking that his greetings be passed to the people he knows in Rome. There are three quite surprising elements to the list. The first is the number of women. This is the answer to those feminists who don't like Paul because they believe he was a misogynist – nothing of the kind! Paul valued women, and he mentions ten of them in the list. That is a high proportion. He had a very large place in his heart as well as in the work for the women who had been his colleagues. The very first, Phoebe, was the woman who had brought the letter all the way from Corinth to Rome. Had she not been faithful with that we would never have had this epistle. Phoebe was a deaconess. An elder is an overseer of the church. A deacon or deaconess is a servant of the church, and she was a wonderful servant as well as a postwoman.

Then look at some of the other names. There is Priscilla and the name means "old-fashioned" and presumably she was so named by her parents. What a name to give a girl. Priscilla was from the top social bracket and was a team with her husband for the Lord. They are always mentioned together. Then there are people like Mary, Junias, Tryphaena and Tryphosa. Names like that always indicate twins. When they had twins in those days they gave them very similar names, either with the first or last part exactly the same, so Tryphaena and Tryphosa were twin girls, twin women. Persis, Rufus's mother; now there we have a connection with the man from Cyrene who carried the cross of Jesus when Jesus fell. There is Julia, Nereus's sister – ten women altogether. Incidentally, "Phoebe" was originally a pagan name so she seems to have come from a pagan background originally. But Phoebe is now a believer and a great helper to Paul and others. She is a support [Greek: *prostatis*; helper]. What a lovely name!

The next surprise in this list is that many of those mentioned were Paul's physical relatives. Paul had been used to evangelise his own family. Do you know that amongst Jesus' twelve disciples, at least five and possibly seven were his own physical relatives? Jesus himself began with his relatives. That is why he was found at the wedding of Cana where he was invited with some of his disciples. They were relatives. Andronicus and Junias were relatives of Paul. Herodion was a relative of Paul, named after King Herod apparently. Apart from the relatives, there were his colleagues – people who served the Lord with Paul in his work. Now most of these would be Jews who had come back to Rome when they were allowed to do so, under Nero.

Now he says a shocking thing: "Kiss them." When you read the words, "Greet them with a holy kiss," did you feel the shock? These are Gentile believers who have begun to think that the Jews were rejected by God and that they have replaced the Jewish people. Kiss the Jews? Yes, kiss them. It is like an electric shock, isn't it? I can imagine when this letter was read in Rome, as it would have been. It would not be duplicated and circulated, it would be read aloud right through in Rome, and when it got to this – "Kiss them" – I could see them looking at each other. It was to be a holy kiss. I think I said earlier that the difference between a kiss and a holy kiss is two minutes, but I can tell you better by telling you what an unholy kiss is. Judas Iscariot gave Jesus an unholy kiss. While he was actually kissing Jesus, he was betraying his best friend to death. That is an unholy kiss, which has gone down into history. Everybody knows about that kiss and Judas, but this time it is to be a holy kiss.

In the next section, vv. 17–20, Paul gives a warning about who *not* to welcome. It is important that a church should welcome many but not welcome some. There is a discipline about entering a church, and some people should be avoided: there are the people who cause division among you – don't welcome them, avoid them. They do it by deception, smooth talk and flattery. The little letter of Jude warns us about people who worm their way into the fellowship and spoil it. I am afraid that is one of the dangers that every church must watch. When you have built a successful fellowship, people will come in and take it over for themselves if they can. I have seen that happen in so many cases. Some of the new fellowships in Britain got off to a good start and then, later, people joined, came in and divided them. Don't welcome everybody. Be wise about whom you welcome in.

Now how do you detect them and deal with them? The answer is to be wise about good things and innocent about evil things. That is almost an echo of, "Wise as serpents; harmless as doves," as Jesus put it.

The next section consists of greetings from where Paul is writing the letter, to the church at Rome. The first group of greetings were to the people in Rome that he knew, and probably who had told him that they were not welcome back. I think Aquila and Priscilla probably put him in the picture about this tension in the church of Rome. Now he is giving greetings from where he is to where they are. Again he mentions colleagues. Timothy was the young man he had mentored and trained – his apprentice, if you like. Timothy was a timid, shy young man. Paul had to teach him how to be bold and how to stir up the gift that was in him, but Paul had done very successfully with Timothy. Though he preached against circumcision, Paul had circumcised young Timothy so that he could go into Jewish homes freely and evangelise Jews. So Paul was adaptable.

He mentions Tertius. Tertius, the man who wrote this letter down. I can imagine what a headache he had with Paul striding up and down in the room and dictating the whole of Romans non-stop. Reading it through non-stop is quite a task, but this man had to write it down. He was feverishly scratching away with a pen while Paul said, "Now write this; now this – Ah, yes, must mention that." Poor Tertius kept up with him and gave us Romans. We can be thankful that Tertius wrote Romans down for us.

Relatives of Paul are mentioned again. He had relatives everywhere! He mentions three of them: Lucius, and you will find all about him in Acts 13; Jason, you find all about him in Acts 17; Sosipater, you find all about him in Acts 20. These are not just names, they are people who played a part in the spread of the gospel. When you know other scriptures you find out more about them. By the way, there was one name, Epaenetus, in the first list of greetings who was Paul's first convert in Asia. What an amazing thing! The very first one. Then there is a man called Ampliatus, and quite recently an archaeologist was digging in an ancient cemetery on the outskirts of Rome and came across his grave. That is the only thing I know about him, but I think that is interesting.

Returning to the greetings from other people, there were also officials. Interestingly, they did get some of the top people. They had the city treasurer of Corinth, a man called Erastus, the city's director of public works. It is great when somebody who is prominent in the public eye and has a responsible position in civic life comes to Christ, but there were very few in those days. Not many noble, not many wise were called. God likes ordinary people. He seems to have a preference for a majority of ordinary folk like us. Gaius was obviously a wealthy and prominent citizen whose house was large enough for a church to meet in, so it must have been quite large. These are noblemen, as we would call them. The brother of Erastus, the city's director of public works, was another, Quartus. It is a fascinating list.

When I began to teach on Romans again, after a gap of some years since the publication of the first edition of my Commentary, which was based on talks given some two decades earlier, how fresh it came and what new thoughts I had! I had no new thoughts that contradicted the thoughts of twenty years earlier, but it came as fresh. I find that Romans is a book that you can read again and again for a whole lifetime and still it is fresh and new. It is almost as if you are reading it for the first time again. Do you know any other book like that?

We conclude where Paul finished – with the doxology. That is the word for praise to God. Paul has already had one doxology in Romans 11. Remember, "For from him and through him and to him..." giving glory to God there, and now he does it again. A doxology is when you give glory to God not so much for what he does but simply for who he is. Paul finishes by praising God for three things. Firstly, that he is *able* to establish us, to make us firm and strong and immovable. He is an able God, and that little word "able" is used again and again in the New Testament. He is able to complete the work that he has begun in you. He is able to do everything he plans and everything he has promised.

Secondly, he is not only able but he has *opened to us*. He reveals mysteries to us. He loves to share secrets with us that the human mind would never have been able to guess. We have heard things in this very letter that no human could ever have discovered with the most brilliant brain in the world, but God has shared the secret – the secret that Israel as a whole will come to God in the end. Nobody would have guessed that.

Thirdly, he is the *only wise God*. That does not mean there are lots of other gods who are foolish, but it is just saying he is the wisest God of all, the only wise God. Now what does that mean? A wise person knows what is the right thing to do and does it. That is my simple definition. He knows the right thing to do and the right way to do it. That is wisdom. He is willing to share that with us, too. To him be glory, forever and ever! Amen.

A brief resumé of Paul's letter

THE RIGHTEOUSNESS OF GOD

Commentators have divided up the epistle in a variety of ways. I could have put these sixteen chapters under three headings: faith, hope and love, Paul's favourite list of three virtues. In fact, chapters 1–4 are concerned with faith, being justified by faith, having faith in God like Abraham. Then chapters 5–11 are concerned with our hope. Chapter 5 begins with a statement of hope and it describes the future that is laid before us: the future of the Jews, the future of the Gentiles, our future hope when the whole creation is set free from its groans and its travails. Then, with chapter 12, we move into love. From there to the end of the epistle, Paul is describing how Christians are to love one another and consider one another as brothers in the same fellowship. It could also be divided down the middle: chapters 1–8 as the salvation that God works *in*, then 9–16 as salvation being worked *out* – first in relation to the Jew and second in relation to the Gentile.

Salvation is a combination of God working something in, and me working something out. There is a combination of his activity and mine, but I cannot work it out until he has worked it in. The trouble is that many people think salvation is working *for* something, but the Bible never tells you to work for your salvation. The Bible only says you work it *out*; God will work it in. You cannot save yourself. God will work it in and then you have to work it out. You have to work it out in your relationships, your conversation and your daily work, your home and family. But you cannot work it out until God has worked it in. Any attempt to work out Christianity before it is being worked in is doomed to failure and will distort and pervert the whole thing.

So chapters 1–8 are concerned with the salvation that God the Holy Trinity works into you. God the Father planned it from all eternity; God the Son came and purchased it for me two thousand years ago; God the Holy Spirit works it into my heart today.

Paul, describing how salvation is worked in, must talk about God the Father in chapters 1–4, about God the Son in chapters five and six, and about God the Holy Spirit in chapters 7–8. The whole logic and pattern of it unfolds before your eyes. Though at first sight, reading it through, the epistle may seem to suggest that Paul is jumping from one subject to another and covering so much ground, there is a divine logic in what he says. Step by step, always in the right order (faith, hope, love) Paul describes the salvation that is ours in Christ Jesus.

Now some crucial little passages. The first is at the end of the greeting in the prologue, 1:16–17.

For I am not ashamed of the gospel; it is the power of God for salvation to everyone who has faith, to the Jew first and also to the Greek, for in it the righteousness of God is revealed through faith, for faith. As it is written, "He who through faith is righteous shall live."

Just as a symphony often begins as well as ends with a crashing chord, here we have this magnificent chord of Christian truth in which there are four notes.

First *the gospel of God*, and the word "God" occurs frequently in this epistle. It is God-centred. The second note in the introductory chord is the power – the "dynamite"– of God. You need never be ashamed of power; the gospel of God is about the power of God. The power of God is to achieve the *righteousness of God* which was his way of putting men right and of putting the world right. The gospel of God, the power of God and the righteousness of God are to be found in the word of God. (Paul gives his text from Habakkuk 2:4 at the end of v. 17.) So here is the gospel that Paul preached, and he says if anyone, from anywhere, at any time, in any place, preaches any other gospel than this let him be accursed – because he will poison men's minds. He will enslave their souls. There is only one gospel that has the power of God and the righteousness of God in it. Therefore, you must always test a preacher by Paul's letter to the Romans. This is the only gospel there is, and even if an angel from heaven should come and preach anything else, don't listen. That angel is mistaken; there is only one good news.

Now let us look at salvation worked *in*. The three parts of the first eight chapters are the righteousness of God, the redemption in Christ Jesus, and the resurrection of new life through the Holy Spirit. The "righteousness of God" can mean one of two things. If God is absolutely righteous, then when he meets sin he must judge it. The first three chapters are about the judgment of God on sinners. The gospel is bad news before it is good news; the gospel must talk about the judgment of God before it can talk about the mercy. The gospel must talk about the wrath of God, the anger of God against sin, before it can talk about the love of God for the sinner.

Therefore, Paul in the first three chapters must diagnose the condition of people in sin before he offers the cure. He must show man's judgment under God's wrath before he can hope to show them God's forgiveness and justification.

In chapter 1 he demonstrates the justice of God's anger by pointing out that even among men who have never heard the gospel, never read the Bible, through the creation around them and the conscience within them they know perfectly well that there is a God and they have no excuse for denying his existence.

Paul, you remember, said about these people all over the world, "They have given God up, so God has given them up." It is absolutely fair and just; there is nothing unfair about God's dealing with mankind. People gave God up for idolatry, so God gave people up to immorality. They suppressed the truth and substituted a lie so God gave them up to debased minds and dishonoured bodies – a diagnosis of secular society that is devastating in its accuracy.

In chapter 2 he went on to the subject of judgment generally. We ask: who, what and how will he judge? Who will he judge? Everyone, whether they say they have sinned or not. He will judge what they have done. He will judge those who on the one hand have done good all the time, 100%, as fit for reward, and those who have not done good all the time as fit for punishment.

How will he judge? He will judge everyone according to the light they have received. If they only had their conscience, then God will say to them, "Did you live up to that conscience?" If they had the Ten Commandments then God will say, "Did you live up to the Ten Commandments?" If they were taught in Sunday school the ethics of our Lord Jesus, then it is by that they will be judged. God will be absolutely fair. He will only say to a man, "What light did you have and did you always live up to it?"

In chapter 3 Paul is addressing Jews who may think they will escape this but will not. Pride and privileges had blinded their eyes to the practice of sin in their own nation. It does not matter who you are, whether Jew or Gentile, whether you have had the Bible or not – the whole world needs forgiveness. The whole world is under sin and the whole world is guilty before God. The whole world justly deserves his wrath.

Now, that is the disease, that is the diagnosis, and that is when he is able to begin the good news. There are many people who don't even think the world is sinful and guilty. But in a devastating, logical manner, Paul has demonstrated that there is not a man or woman on earth can stand before God and say, "God I have always lived up to the light I received; I have always done what I knew to be right; I have shaped my life according to the good that I knew."

The good news is that God has found quite a different way of putting us right. Instead of saying to us, "You must put yourself right and then come to me," God now says, "I am going to put you right so that you can come to me." That is the difference between Christianity and every other religion in the world, including Judaism. The other religions tell you how to put yourself right and then come to God. The tragedy is that it is like telling a man to lift himself by pulling on his bootlaces. You can't! But God says: I am going to put you right. I am going to give you my righteousness instead of leaving you to try and find some of your own. I am going to make you good instead of leaving you to make yourself good. It is as simple as that.

Martin Luther, struggling with Paul's letter to the Romans saw this phrase "the righteousness of God" and could not think what it meant. He thought it meant that God will punish me, that God will send me to hell for my sins. It does mean that, but he couldn't see anything more. Then one day the light shone in his monastery cell. One day he saw its truth. One day he realised that the righteousness of God is his righteousness not mine, and it is a righteousness that he wants to give me. His chains fell off, his heart was free, and the Reformation had begun – because a man realised that the new way to be right with God, the new way to be good, is not to try to be good, not to try to keep the commandments, but to receive by simple faith the righteousness of God as a free gift. That is the good news.

In 3:21–26 we have another passage you should learn. It is the heart of the epistle:

But now a righteousness from God has been manifested apart from the law, although the law and the prophets bear witness to it, the righteousness of God, through faith in Jesus Christ for all who believe. For there is no distinction since all have sinned and fall short of the glory of God. They are justified by his grace as a gift through the redemption which is in Christ Jesus, whom God put forward as an expiation by his blood, to be received by faith. This was to show God's righteousness because in his divine forbearance he had passed over former sins. It was to prove at the present time that he himself is righteous and that he justifies him who has faith in Jesus.

There are three wonderful notes here: his righteousness revealed, his grace given, his perfection proved. The only way God could prove that he was *just* and *merciful* was at the cross. The only place at which God could be both perfectly at the same time was at Calvary by punishing the innocent for the guilty. Only in that way could sin be punished and the sinner pardoned; there was no other way.

Chapter 4 describes more fully the faith required to receive such a gift, and builds around the life of Abraham a picture of a man of faith who believed that God can do the impossible, who believed that God can bring something out of nothing, who believed that God could raise from the dead; a man who believed where he could not see and threw his whole future into the unknown at God's command; a man who, at the age of eighty, trusted God implicitly with everything he had. Paul is saying that if you can have the faith that Abraham had in God, but if you can put it in God through Christ, then you will find what he found, that God forgives the man who has faith.

So much for the righteousness of God in chapters 1–4. You will have it one of these two ways: you will either meet the righteousness of God as judgment on the sinner, or you will receive it as justification, being put right, getting into God's good books through faith in Christ Jesus. Every single person in creation will meet the righteousness of God as a judgment or as a gift – believers meet the righteousness of God as pardon; unbelievers meet it as punishment. Either way, God must be righteous.

In chapters 5 and 6 we come to "the redemption that is in Christ Jesus". "Redemption" is a word from the marketplace meaning liberation, buying something back; to redeem is to rescue something from someone else's ownership and have it for yourself. To be redeemed is to be bought and then set free. When you have had faith in Christ for forgiveness you are in fact set free from two things: from sin's *penalty* of death (chapter 5 develops that theme) and from the dominion of sin's *power*. There is a glorious description of the experience of a person who has faith in God through Christ:

Therefore, since we are justified by faith, we have peace with God through our Lord Jesus Christ. Through him, we have obtained access to this grace in which we stand and we rejoice in our hope of sharing the glory of God. More than that, we rejoice in our sufferings, knowing that suffering produces endurance, and endurance produces character, and character produces hope. And hope does not disappoint us because God's love has been poured into our hearts through the Holy Spirit which has been given to us.

Here is the peace of faith through Christ, the patience of hope in God, and the pouring of love in the Holy Spirit. The rest of chapter 5 deals with the death of sin's penalty. Describing the Son of God's death and his living again, Paul then goes on to describe the sons of men in their death and in their resurrection and living again.

At this point Paul explains that what happened to Adam at the beginning of the human race affected everybody else in it – everybody dies because one man sinned. Only if you accept that can you accept the other side of the truth: that because one man died, everybody may live. If you cannot accept that the whole human race is sinful because one man sinned, and dies because one man sinned, you will never understand how you could live because Jesus died.

But just as Adam's single act of disobedience led a whole race of people who were in Adam to die, so the one act of obedience in Christ led to a whole new race of people who are in Christ, living for ever. That's how Jesus conquered sin's penalty, by introducing into the human race a new act which would affect everybody who was going to be in Christ, just as Adam affected everybody who was in Adam. As in Adam, we all die, so in Christ, we shall all be made alive—that deals with death. When Christ died, death died. When Christ died, death lost its sting and its grip on me, and because I am in Christ I live and will live for ever.

A Christian, reading Romans 5, has no fear of physical death. He knows that it is not death, it is to go to be with the Lord in glory, which is far better. My death came as the result of the guilt of Adam's sin; my life comes as the result of the gift of Christ's righteousness. Adam's disobedience causes me to die; Christ's obedience brings me life. Whereas death is wages, life is a gift. I have worked for my death and indeed, my sins are always working for my death, but I have received life as a gift – that is Romans 5.

So when Christ died, you got life, and Romans 6 goes even further. When Christ died, you died. I believe that when Christ hung on the cross, I died. That wonderful truth you can prove in your experience. The principle is that you died on the cross with Christ. The practice of that principle is: reckon yourself dead and sin will have no dominion over you. Tell the devil that you died on a cross, tell the devil he can't touch you now, and you will find that is the sober truth. Reckon yourselves dead, therefore. Present your members to God, to righteousness. Your slavery in sin has been smashed; your chains have gone because the one thing you cannot do is to tempt a dead man.

At the cross, Jesus Christ not only obtained our pardon and freedom from the guilt and *penalty* of sin, but obtained our freedom from the *power* of it. He smashed the power of Satan because in Christ I died and every Christian died. You will find that it is true. Sin will have no more dominion over you if you can just realise that when Christ died you did. You were *crucified* with Christ; you were *buried* with him in baptism, you were *raised* with him to newness of life. Don't you realise that you have gone through it all? That you are the other side of the resurrection morning now? Just as the enemies of Christ could not touch him after he came out of the tomb, the devil can't touch you now if you realise this: you are dead, and sin has no more dominion over you. That is the redemption that is in Christ Jesus. Chapter 5—he set me free from sin's penalty – death. Chapter 6, he has set me free from sin's dominion, sin's power. Isn't that a redemption worth singing about? He died that you might be forgiven; he died to make you good, that you might go at last to heaven, saved by his precious blood. The cross did for us what we needed. It set us free from the penalty; it broke the power.

That has already brought us on to the resurrection and the new life in Christ Jesus. Chapters 7 and 8 belong together and they contrast the old life and the new life in the Spirit, the resurrection life, the life that comes from the Spirit of him who raised up Jesus from the dead, dwelling in us.

Chapter 7 is that very sad and disturbing chapter of a man who has on the one hand a deceived soul and, on the other, a divided self – and all because he let the law tell him what to do. The trouble was that when the law told him what to do, he thought, "If I do that, I'll get to heaven." It deceived him and he couldn't do it. His mind wanted to serve the Lord God, but his members didn't. Telling you that you are dead, and that sin should no longer have dominion over you (chapter 6) is not enough, for we know perfectly well that it often does. Another positive power is needed. It is not enough for the power of sin to be taken away. I still haven't the power in myself to get free. The power of the Holy Spirit is needed. If someone's past sins are forgiven, they still need a power that will take the place of the power of sin, because in our flesh there is no good thing. In the flesh I am weak. My mind wants to serve the Lord God, but my members don't. The good I would, I do not; the evil that I would not, that I do. Who hasn't cried out like that? Christians can cry that out as much as unbelievers.

The answer is in chapter 8. There is a new resurrection life, power in the Spirit. The relief of chapter 8 is that there is now neither *condemnation* for my sin nor *compulsion* to sin – because the law of the Spirit of life has set me free from the law of sin and death. The whole of the chapter is about the new life of the Holy Spirit, pulsating life. I have a new Father, whereby I cry, "Abba". I have a new future, whereby I groan in travail, waiting for that redeeming act of God whereby he sets us free.

Even now while I am groaning for that new future, the Holy Spirit helps me in my weakness and teaches me how to pray. Life in the Spirit – no longer need I be in the flesh, for the way of the flesh is death and war. The Spirit brings me to life and peace. The flesh drags me down; the Spirit lifts me up. The flesh would lead me into death; the Spirit brings life. The flesh chains me; the Spirit gives me liberty. Either way, I am insufficient by myself. By myself, I serve the law of sin and death; in the Spirit, I serve the law of God. It is no use breaking the power of sin in someone's life if you cannot replace that with the power of the Spirit. It is like sweeping someone clean of evil spirits and leaving the house empty for other evil spirits to come back in.

At the end of the passage: "We know that all things work together for good to them that love God...." God's sovereignty is my security because he is in charge of all things, so then I need fear nothing. Because he is in charge of all people, then I need fear no people. We finish with that magnificent statement that I am persuaded, absolutely sure, neither death nor life, angels, principalities, powers, things present, things to come, height, depth, any other creature, shall be able to separate us from the love of God which is in Christ Jesus.

But weren't the Jews separated? Didn't they lose it? We are right into the next section of the letter. Salvation worked in; now let us see – first, in relation to the Jews; second, in relation to the Gentiles—how it is all going to work out. Paul deals with the Jews in chapters 9–11 and we can roughly divide it by those three chapters. In chapter 9 he deals with their past rejection; in chapter 10 their present responsibility; and in chapter 11 their future restoration. Here is the history of the Jews in a nutshell. Paul's sorrow, his concern for them, is matched by God's sovereignty. God rejected them; God was free to do so. He is the potter; we are the clay. God could take Abraham and Isaac; he could take Moses and make him a vessel of mercy, and take Pharaoh and make him a vessel of wrath.

Why did God do it? The answer is at the end of chapter 9. Because he had ordained that not all inside Israel should be saved and not all outside Israel should be lost. This comes out in quotations from Hosea and Isaiah. Their present responsibility before God is this: there is a double failure in the Jewish people. On the one hand, they have failed to achieve righteousness; on the other, they have failed to receive the revelation. They failed to achieve righteousness because they thought it was achieved by keeping the commandments, not by faith in the Lord. They failed to receive the revelation because, though it came to them, they heard it but did not heed it. They understood it, but they did not undertake it. It all comes out in Romans 10. That is their present responsibility. Of course, they must hear. We must send missionaries. How shall they hear without a preacher? But chapter 11 opens a glorious future when they are to be restored as a nation to the Lord; they are to be brought back. In the past, some Jews believed; in the present, many Gentiles believe; in the future, "all Israel" will be saved. That is God's plan.

Turning from the Jew to the Gentile, the sanctification of the Christians is now worked out. In chapter 12: our bearing in the world. We are not to be chameleons, we are to be caterpillars. A chameleon takes its colour from the outside environment. It is conformed to things around it. The caterpillar is transformed from within by the process of metamorphosis, and the beauty of the butterfly's wings is formed from within, not from without. Don't be conformed to your world, but be "metamorphosed" like the caterpillar, from within, and let the beauty come out. Have your mind transformed from within. Don't be conformed in outer behaviour to the world. Our *attitude to God* is to present our bodies in worship, a reasonable sacrifice, and to present our minds for the will of God. Our *attitude to ourselves* is that we will not think more highly than we ought to think, and that we will have useful works added to our faith. Our *attitude to others* is that we will have fellowship with friends and will exercise forgiveness to our enemies – that is chapter 12. In the world, we are to have a right attitude to God, a right attitude to ourselves, a right attitude to others.

Chapter 13 concerns our behaviour in the state. We are to have a particular attitude to the rulers above us – not bad deeds, but loyalty. To the neighbours around us: no bad debts, the debt of love. Of the passions within us: no bad desires, just light, walking as children of the light.

Chapter 14 and part of chapter 15 concern our brotherhood in the church – that between a weak and a strong brother, the weak brother who has scruples and the strong brother, who by his more libertarian behaviour could put stumbling blocks in the way of the weak brother, particularly in matters of diet and days. It is so easy for Christians to fall out over behaviour. Our brotherhood means that the strong brother considers the weak, and adjusts his behaviour accordingly.

In chapter 16 we are reminded of the communion of saints. The church is people – ordinary believers, not just the great, well-known ones like Paul.

Books by David Pawson available from www.davidpawsonbooks.com

A Commentary on the Gospel of Mark
A Commentary on the Gospel of John
A Commentary on Acts
A Commentary on Romans
A Commentary on Galatians
A Commentary on 1 & 2 Thessalonians
A Commentary on Hebrews
A Commentary on James
A Commentary on The Letters of John
A Commentary on Jude
A Commentary on the Book of Revelation
By God, I Will (The Biblical Covenants)
Angels
Christianity Explained
Come with me through Isaiah
Defending Christian Zionism
Explaining the Resurrection
Explaining the Second Coming
Explaining Water Baptism
Is John 3:16 the Gospel?
Israel in the New Testament
Jesus Baptises in One Holy Spirit
Jesus: The Seven Wonders of HIStory
Kingdoms in Conflict
Leadership is Male
Living in Hope
Not as Bad as the Truth (autobiography)
Once Saved, Always Saved?
Practising the Principles of Prayer
Remarriage is Adultery Unless....
Simon Peter: The Reed and the Rock
The Challenge of Islam to Christians
The Character of God
The God and the Gospel of Righteousness
The Lord's Prayer
The Maker's Instructions (Ten Commandments)
The Normal Christian Birth
The Road to Hell
Unlocking the Bible
What the Bible says about the Holy Spirit
When Jesus Returns
Where has the Body been for 2000 years?
Where is Jesus Now?
Why Does God Allow Natural Disasters?
Word and Spirit Together

Unlocking the Bible
is also available in DVD format from www.davidpawson.com

Lightning Source UK Ltd.
Milton Keynes UK
UKHW02f2108210318
319853UK00012B/482/P